Mystic Martyr

Memories from the Life of Aḥmad ʿAlī Nayrī

A Multi-Authored Biography

AL-BURĀQ

Copyright

ISBN: 978-1-956276-54-1
Printed and published by al-Burāq Publications.
Translated by Brother Amir Ḥusayn and edited by Hoda Fakhari. Where needed, context and transliterations were added. Some minor edits were made to the translated text.

Ordering Information
We offer discounts and promotions for wholesale purchases, non-profit organizations, and other educational institutions. Contact us at the email below for further information.

www.al-Buraq.org
publications@al-Buraq.org

First Edition | October 2024

Dedication

The publication of this book was made possible through the generous support of our donors.

Please recite *Sūrat al-Fātihah* and ask God for the Divine reward (*thawāb*) to be conferred upon the donors and also the souls of all the deceased in whose memory their loved ones have contributed graciously towards the publication of *Mystic Martyr: Memories from the Life of Aḥmad ʿAlī Nayrī*.

We begin by giving all praise and thanks to God ﷻ for giving us the *tawfīq* to translate this book. He has guided us and without Him, we would not have been guided to the straight path embodied by the Prophet Muḥammad ﷺ and the Ahl al-Bayt عليهم السلام.

This book is dedicated to all the scholars, martyrs and believers who worked tirelessly to promote the pure Muḥammadan path.

We want to also give our thanks and appreciation to all believers from around the world and acknowledge the team which helped al-Burāq Publications complete this work, spending countless hours to make its publication possible. Please recite Sūrat al-Fātiḥah on behalf of them, their families, and their marḥūmīn.

Lastly, this book is dedicated in honor of Shahīd Aḥmad ʿAlī Nayrī and his family. Please remember them in your prayers and may God ﷻ have mercy on them and their loved ones.

Duʿāʾ al-Ḥujjah

اللهم كن لوليك الحجة بن الحسن صلواتك
عليه وعلى آبائه في هذه الساعة وفي كل
ساعة وليا وحافظا وقائدا وناصرا ودليلا
وعينا حتى تسكنه أرضك طوعا وتمتعه فيها طويلا

O God, be, for Your representative, the Ḥujjat (proof), son of al-Ḥasan, Your blessings be upon him and his forefathers, in this hour and in every hour: a guardian, a protector, a leader, a helper, a proof, and an eye—until You make him live on the Earth, in obedience (to You), and cause him to live in it for a long time.

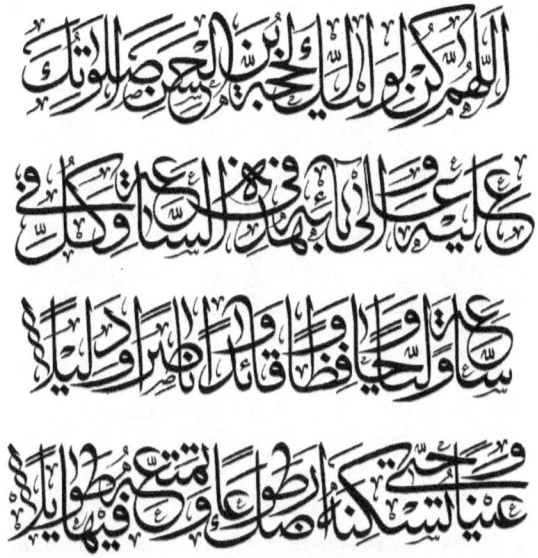

Terms of Respect

The following Arabic phrases have been used throughout this book in their respective places to show the reverence which the noble personalities deserve.

عزّ وجلّ

Used for God, meaning:
Exalted and Sublime (Perfect) is He

صلّى الله عليه وآله

Used for Prophet Muḥammad, meaning:
Blessings from God be upon him and his family

عليه السلام

Used for a man (singular) of a high status, meaning:
Peace be upon him

عليها السلام

Used for a woman (singular) of a high status, meaning:
Peace be upon her

عليهما السلام

Used for men/women (dual) of a high status, meaning:
Peace be upon them both

عليهم السلام

Used for men and/or women (plural) of a high status, meaning:
Peace be upon them all

عجّل الله تعالى فرجه الشريف

Used for Imām Muḥammad al-Mahdī, meaning:
May God hasten his return

قدّس سرّه

Used for a deceased scholar, meaning:
May his resting [burial] place remain pure

Transliteration Table

The method of transliteration of Islāmic terminology from the Arabic language has been carried out according to the standard transliteration table below.

ء	ʾ	ر	r	ف	f
ا	a	ز	z	ق	q
ب	b	س	s	ك	k
ت	t	ش	sh	ل	l
ث	th	ص	ṣ	م	m
ج	j	ض	ḍ	ن	n
ح	ḥ	ط	ṭ	و	w
خ	kh	ظ	ẓ	ه	h
د	d	ع	ʿ	ي	y
ذ	dh	غ	gh		
Long Vowels					
ا	ā	و	ū	ي	ī
Short Vowels					
ـَ	a	ـُ	u	ـِ	i

Table of Contents

Disclaimer

This publication is not affiliated with, influenced by, or funded by any domestic or foreign political entities. It is intended purely for historical record-keeping due to the lack of accessible Farsi texts for a Western audience. This text is aimed at academics and historians alike, providing valuable insights into the subject matter. The contents do not represent our views or opinions, nor do they endorse any specific ideologies or perspectives presented. While every effort has been made to ensure the accuracy and relevance of the selected texts, the publication may not include all viewpoints. The material reflects the historical context at the time of writing and should be understood as such.

Aḥmad Āghā

بسم الله الرحمن الرحيم

In the Name of God, the Beneficent, the Merciful

"Whoever is absent from this circle, living for love's sake,

Even in their life, according to my decree, offer the funeral prayer."

We have become accustomed to it. Our lives have become automatic machines that repeatedly take us from morning to night, day after day! It has been a long time since we have made time for ourselves. We used to ponder a little about the past, the future, God ﷻ, qiyāmah (resurrection), etc., but now, television and other media, along with self-made occupations, have also taken away the opportunity for thinking.

What are we doing? Where are we going? Lest science, technology, and other tools of civilization shackled us with desire, anger, and lust. Lest the days pass, and our only savings from this world are missed opportunities. Lest we ultimately depart from this ruin empty-handed and embark on a journey [back to our Lord] without a path, lest we never even know why we had come in the first place.

After all, if our entire purpose in being on this planet is the same as what has been mentioned, then what is the difference between us and...

Sayyid Shahīdān from Qalam said, "If the goal is to fly, then the cage is better [left] as a ruin. When a swallow sees flying as the goal, he is not afraid of the destruction of his nest... And if there is no ladder from the earth to the sky, then only fat and self-indulgent worms will develop."

Thus, shouldn't we consider building our house there if we ascend from this ruin to our eternal abode? Is it not that here, the houses are unstable, the abodes are eternal, and we are travelers on a journey, so why do we pass our lives in negligence? Why is the control of our lives entrusted to Shayṭān (the devil)? Why don't we allocate time for ourselves?

Why don't our prayers and worship have the slightest effect on our īmān (faith)? Moreover, there are hundreds of other reasons we do not even have the opportunity to contemplate for ourselves.

***

In this collection, we wish to present one of the excellent personalities of this Ummah—one who lived alongside us, leading a life similar to ours yet simple and unpretentious. He lived his entire life with purpose. He did not entrust himself to the whims of daily life. He looked at life differently and made the most of every moment. He was an "ʿabd (servant)" in every sense. Life and its physical beauty could not deceive him.

He used every material resource at his disposal as a bridge to perfection, to achieve the purpose of creation, to reach the Divine. This young man lived near us, south of the city beside the Māwlavi Bāzār. Although, I am not talking about ancient times! I am not a fan of myths or creating legends, either. I am talking about someone who lived among us in contemporary times.

He lived like us, the way we do now. He studied and worked. He lived life casually and, in the same manner, packed up his belongings and left for the final destination. He was so simple and unpretentious that no one [properly] recognized him—not even his family! No one truly figured out who he truly was.

However, the difference between him and the likes of us was his "yaqīn (certainty)." He recognized the path. He understood what he needed to pursue in this world. He had a plan for every minute of his life. His life was what God ﷻ had ordained for human beings. He ascended the stairs of perfection one after the other and increased his distance from the people of this world.

He would say, "Why are you like this? Rise higher, come, and see what is worth seeing! Why have you tied your heart to this ruin? Why?" He would speak, and we, the sleepy ones in the arms of negligence, just watched him! As time passed, his inner radiance of his being left had a greater impact on his words and actions, for he was not a captive of the traps of this world. He would speak to us of the above. If you work for God ﷻ and have sincerity, the fountains of divine wisdom will flow towards you.

Moreover, we were certain he had drunk from the fountains of divine wisdom with all his being. He belonged to the heavens and had no business with the world's people. However, his heart ached for us. He would say, "One day, we must leave this abode—so why haven't we prepared to travel?" But we should have [truly] appreciated him when he, like other virtuous individuals, ascended to the heavens with the caravan of the martyrs.

Even when his body was carried through the bāzār and mosque, still no one [truly] recognized him. Some scholars say, "Only one person recognized him, and he was the one who nūrtured this youth in his lap: the teachers of the Mystics, Āyat al-Ḥaqq Āyatullāh Ḥaqq-Shinās."

When the people saw that he attended the funeral ceremony, visited the house of this martyr, and spoke of some aspects of his personality for him, only then did they begin to understand what a gem they had just lost!

Āyatullāh Ḥaqq-Shinās recounted the miraculous deeds and qualities of this sincere servant of God ﷻ and said, "Alas, alas, Āghā, wander around Tehrān. Can you find someone like Aḥmad Āghā?"

Indeed, Aḥmad Āghā accompanied us for nineteen springs to teach us how to live and traverse this earthly realm. May his memory be honored!

You Whom I Never Understood

Where has this torn rose come from? It came from the trip to Karb and Balā'.

Today is the third of Esfand[1], 1364 (February 22, 1986). The crowd chanted this slogan as they carried the martyr's body from the front of his house to Masjid Amīn al-Dawlah. Then, accompanied by the crowd, we headed to Māwlavi Bāzār. This crowd, mostly mosque youths and students of Āyatullāh Ḥaqq-Shinās cried intensely and were overwhelmed with grief.

I had been attending the services of Ḥajj Āghā Ḥaqq-Shinās, a teacher of ethics and the path of God ﷺ, for some time, and I benefited from the fruitful sessions of this master. Before this, I searched for years to find a spiritual teacher. Only with the help of the 'Ulamā' Rabbānī

---

[1] This is the name of the last month in the Persian calendar, corresponding to March.

(Divine Scholars) of Tehrān could I arrive in the presence of this self-made sage. Afterward, I heard that the eminent teacher adored this student very much, so I decided to participate in the funeral ceremony of this beloved martyr. When the ceremony came to an end, they took the martyr's body to the Behesht-e-Zahrā ﷺ cemetery. I went along with them.

Since the martyr fell in battle, he was prepared for burial without a ghusl (ritual washing) or a shroud—just his military uniform. A spot was chosen for him several rows above the grave of the mystic soldier, Shahīd Chamrān. I stepped forward in order to get a glance at the martyr's face. As the door of his coffin opened, I witnessed his innocent and lovable face. He looked lively and beautiful as if he had fallen into a deep sleep! His face bore no resemblance to someone who had departed from this world. His friends said, "It has only been six days since his martyrdom!"

The hand of this martyr was placed in the position of respect on his chest! One of his comrades said, "At the moment of his martyrdom, an explosive hit his side. He asked us to lift him when he fell to the ground. When he stood on his feet, facing towards Karbalā', he placed his hand on his chest and said, 'Peace be upon you, O Abā 'Abdillāh!'" And with these words on his tongue, he departed from this world to meet his shroud less Master. That is why his hand is still placed in the position of respect on his chest!

It seemed strange to me. Why did the seminarians and students of Ustādh Ḥaqq-Shinās, who were otherwise very patient people, lose their composure in the departure of this friend?

They placed the martyr's body inside the grave and started setting the tombstones. The person who placed the final tombstone came out; he was pale! So, I asked, "Has something happened?" He replied, "When I replaced the last stone, a sudden aroma of perfume filled the air in the grave. This scent differed from any earthly fragrance."

Today is the funeral ceremony of the martyr. Some friends notified me that Ustādh Ḥaqq-Shinās would be present at the ceremony! The departure of this young man was especially hard for him.

I stood near the entrance of Masjid Amīn al-Dawlah. I wanted to enter with the Ustādh. A few minutes later, this godly man appeared from one of the alleyways and approached the mosque with some of his students.

Once before the mosque door, the old soul raised his head and glanced at the bystanders. Then, with a mournful and gloomy tone, he said, "Alas, alas, Āghā Jān..."

Again, taking a wistful sigh, he said, "Wander around Tehrān. Can you find someone like Aḥmad Āghā?"

Night fell, and it was time for the evening prayer. On Monday nights and Friday evenings, he [Ustādh Ḥaqq-Shinās] would have gatherings to deliver sermons. A chair was placed for him, and this venerable man would begin his speech.

That night, he did not give his sermon between the two prayers, but he rose from his place and sat in the chair. Then he began to speak. The topic of his speech was regarding this very martyr. Towards the end of this speech, he again let out a wistful and painful sigh for the passing of this martyr. Then, concerning the greatness and status of this martyr, he stated, "I saw him in my dreams last night. I asked Aḥmad, 'How are you?' To which he replied, 'All the things they say about barzakh and the stages after death is true; from the first night of the grave, the questioning and so on; but they took me without any accounting.'"

He paused and continued, "Friends, even Āyatullāh Burūjirdī had an accounting done of him. I do not know what this youth has done to reach the station he reached."

I listened in astonishment to the words of the Ustādh; what had this young man done that the great master of ethics and mysticism would speak of him in such a manner?

After the ceremony, I asked one of the martyr's friends, "How old was he?"

He replied, "Nineteen years old!."[2]

"What did he do in this mosque? Was he a student?"

---

[2] Aḥmad ʿAlī Nayrī, at nineteen, symbolizes the involvement of the youth in the Irān-ʿIrāq War, reflecting the Irānian society's mobilization during the conflict.

He answered, "No, he was not formally a student, but he was one of the students of ethics and mysticism of the esteemed Ustādh. He participated in educational work here and took admissions for the Basīj (Volunteer Forces)[3]."

My astonishment grew even more. How could a nineteen-year-old youth reach such a stature that the Ustādh would speak of him in such a manner?

Later that night, along with a few friends and His Holiness Āyatullāh Ḥaqq-Shinās, we went to the home of the martyr on the north side of the mosque.

As Ḥajj Āghā entered the house, he stopped at the entrance and turned to look at the brother of the martyr. Then, sorrowfully, they recalled a memory saying, "Other than the Khādim (Keeper) of the mosque and I, this honorable martyr also had a key to the mosque." Taking another breath, he added, "I went to the mosque half an hour earlier than the prayer time. As soon as I opened the door, I saw someone praying in the mosque." The eminent Ustādh paused for a moment and continued, "I saw a young man in prostration, but not on the ground! Rather, he glorified the Almighty between the earth and the heavens!"

---

[3] The Basīj, officially known as the Basīj Resistance Force, is a paramilitary organization in Irān, established in 1979 following the Islāmic Revolution. It is part of the Islāmic Revolutionary Guard Corps (IRGC) and is primarily tasked with mobilizing volunteers for various purposes, including civil defense, social welfare, and the enforcement of Islāmic values. The Basīj plays a significant role in Irān's internal security and can be involved in various activities, from community services to military operations.

Ḥajj Āghā Ḥaqq-Shinās, with a tear glistening in his eye, continued: I approached and saw Aḥmad engaged in prayer. When he finished, he came next to me and said, 'So long as I live, do not mention this to anyone.'"

Upon confirmation from Āyatullāh Ḥaqq-Shinās, some of this martyr's closest friends began to speak. They recounted only what they had witnessed with their own eyes, and I listened in astonishment. Was it possible for a young man to attain such a degree of human perfection?

***

I do not know why! Why did I unconsciously find myself in all the ceremonies of this martyr? Why did I hear these strange words from this pious and enlightened scholar? Why? This time, it is a responsibility on our shoulders. Perhaps God ﷻ wants one of His sincere and anonymous servants who lived a simple and ordinary life among us to be introduced to others. In this day and age, where most of humanity is caught up in its animalistic instincts, Aḥmad Āghā becomes a role model for those who seek to traverse the path of servitude. Although decades have passed since his martyrdom, with God's help, we have decided to gather the memories of this divinely elevated 'abd (servant). As we embarked on this endeavor, we realized the challenges ahead.

Aḥmad Āghā was much greater than what we had imagined.

However, if the teacher of mystics (Āyatullāh Ḥaqq-Shinās) had not spoken about him with such praise, the work would have been much harder.

What students and friends mentioned about his miracles and spiritual states made the work harder. Did we have to compile and publish their accounts too?

Do people have the capacity to accept these accounts? Will we be accused of making up fantasies? And just like that, hundreds of other questions I had no answer to occupied my mind. In short, his memories occupied our minds for a while. With God's help, we sought assistance from Aḥmad Āghā himself and began the work. Even if nobody benefits from this book, they are useful for the writer. His story is all about living righteously.

Aḥmad Āghā was the cultural instructor of the mosque. He repeatedly advised his students to act according to religion's commandments and abstain from sin. In many cases, he also taught them the consequences of their actions, the punishments associated with sins, and the virtues of good deeds. He was like a physician curing the spiritual ailments and pains of others. His prescriptions were by religion, the Noble Qur'ān, and aḥadīth (narrations). For this reason, we can still, with trust, look at the touching words of this teacher and position them as a guiding light.

We sought help from God ﷻ and asked for assistance from this martyr's noble spirit. But it was necessary to document his mystical and strange stories. It would not be as interesting if we only included people's memories. This time, our martyr himself helped us! When we were beginning to collect the stories, we received a report!

After 27 years, a small notebook belonging to Aḥmad Āghā was discovered in an old bag pocket. Aḥmad Āghā wrote down some spiritual events and experiences in his handwriting in this notebook. These notes confirmed all the memories of the martyr's friends and the lessons taught about him by Ustādh Ḥaqq-Shinās.

Now, the martyr himself had presented us with a strong source of evidence, so we said bismillāh and continued the work with resolve. We must tell future generations which role models to follow to live a proper life. We have to discuss who they were and how they found the way. We must introduce these stars to future generations so they may better understand this path, God-willing.

Back in the Day

Narrated by the Martyr's Mother

Tehrān was much smaller than what it is now. People had simple but pleasant lives. They were content with little, yet goodness and blessings flowed into their lives. God ﷻ knows that even though the people's economic situation was much worse than now, they were happier. Every time a door opened, a troop of children of all ages flooded the streets and alleys! Homes were small and crowded but filled with blessings and kindness. Early in the morning, the men said Bismillāh and headed out to work; the women stayed home, occupied with cooking and cleaning. Ḥajj Maḥmūd (the martyr's father) and I were born in the village of Āyīneh Varzān in Damāvand. Fate brought us to Tehrān, where we settled around the Māwlavi Bāzār. Ḥajji had a tea shop at the intersection of Cyrus Square (Meydān-e Sīrūs). Back then, most shopkeepers lived near the bāzār to be close to their workplaces. God ﷻ opened the door of His mercy to us, granting us a good life with eight kids. In those years, we would take the children to Damāvand and stay in the village for three months in the summertime. The children enjoyed being away from home and the bustling atmosphere of the bāzār, relishing the nature and climate of the village. We had an apple orchard there, and most relatives lived nearby.

In the summer of 1966, we went to the village again. I was pregnant at the time. In the last days of July, with the help of a midwife, our last child was born: a beautiful boy who became the youngest member of our family.

I wanted to name him Vahīd, but Ḥajji insisted on naming him Aḥmad ʿAlī. Aḥmad ʿAlī stood out from my other children from the very first day. He was a very calm boy, never causing stress, trouble, or fuss. I loved him dearly. He was quiet and never a bother to others. From a young age, he minded his own business. Inside the house, the other eight children acted as guides for Aḥmad. In addition, Ḥajji Maḥmūd did not fall short in the kids' upbringing either. He always took the children to the mosque with him. Ḥajj Maḥmūd was among the God-conscious businessmen trained under the guidance of Shaykh Muḥammad-Ḥusayn Zāhid and Āyatullāh Ḥaqq-Shinās. He was the type of person who performed all his prayers in the mosque.

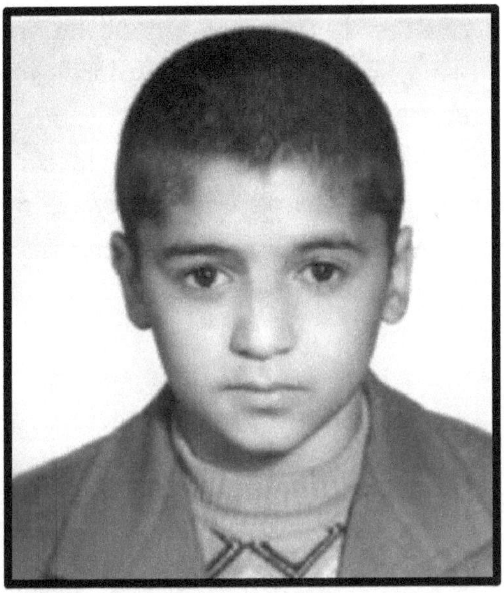

School

The Martyr's Sister

Aḥmad was truly a role model in our family. Everyone loved him. When he turned six years old, we enrolled him in elementary school. The school was called Kazemieh Islāmic School, located around the Lotī Ṣāliḥ Pass. He did well in school, and we never had any issues.

The entire family observed *Namāz Awwal Waqt* (on-time prayers) and Taqwā (God-conscious). Aḥmad paid special attention to worship and spiritual matters, especially prayer, from a young age. Like all other teenagers, he played with his siblings and friends, studied and did school work, and helped with household chores. However, as he grew older, Aḥmad carefully implemented the ethics and behaviors taught in Islām and learned from his elders.

For instance, when he went to school, he would help classmates struggling financially as much as possible. Aḥmad hesitated when we prepared delicious and large meals, and everyone got ready to eat! He said, "In this neighborhood, many people cannot afford such food. People here even have trouble preparing ordinary meals, let alone this..."

That is why, even if he did come to eat, he did so reluctantly. These concerns were very mature for kids his age. Most children in elementary school did not even think of such matters, but Aḥmad discussed them due to the strong insight he picked up from the mosque and the pulpit. That is why the first sparks of perfection were ignited within him during those days.

Every week, as he grew older, so did his growth, perfection, and spirituality – to the point that he reached a position that we could not even compare to the dust of his feet!

We searched for a good school for Aḥmad's middle school education. At that time, there was a peak of anti-religious activities under the Pahlavī regime, so my father sought everyone's help to enter a good school. With the help and guidance of his friends, my father enrolled Aḥmad in the Ḥāfiz School. There, alongside regular school subjects, they would focus on ethical and spiritual lessons, and to some extent, they distanced themselves from the anti-religious issues pushed by the government. The principal and vice principal were religious and had great teachers. Each of them somehow had a role in the kids' spiritual growth.

Ḥusayn Āghā, our elder brother, studied in the Hawza (Islāmic seminary) during that period. He greatly influenced the spiritual atmosphere inside the house as well. In such conditions, Aḥmad worked harder to acquire higher levels of spirituality. I remember once we went to our village in Damāvand to pick apples. Our mother brought a stick from our uncle's farm and started picking apples. A few hours later, our uncle arrived. Aḥmad went forward and greeted him. Then he said, "Uncle, we took a stick from your farm. Please permit us and be content with it." To tease him a little, our uncle responded, "I am not content." Aḥmad kept insisting, "Uncle, please, for the sake of God, please forgive us..." But our uncle would respond even more seriously, "No!" That day, Aḥmad's insistence and our uncle's reaction displayed Aḥmad's sensitivity to the rights of others from a very young age.

In the following years, Aḥmad transferred to Marvī High School and became one of their distinguished students in mathematics. However, he never completed his education. In 1982, while Aḥmad was midway into his second year of mathematics, he decided to drop out!

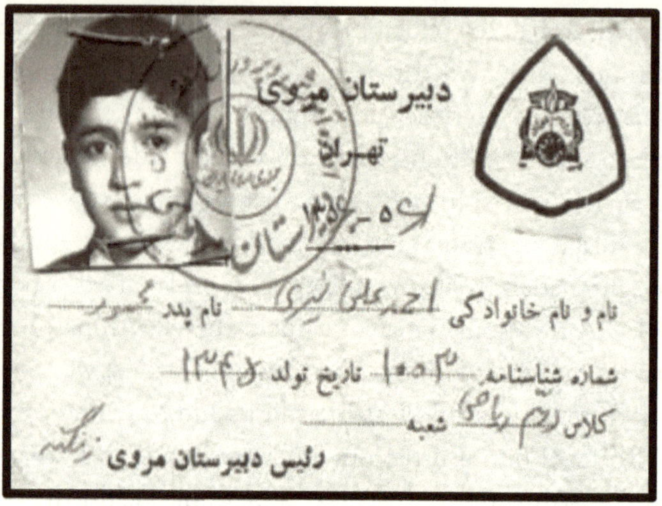

The Test

Dr. Muḥsin Nūrī (Teacher at Shahīd Beheshtī University)

We have been together in the neighborhood since childhood. Aḥmad ʿAlī's house was in Chehel Tan Alley, on the north side of the Amīn al-Dawlah Mosque, a street now renamed "Shahīdan Nayrī." During our time in elementary school, Aḥmad's nature and temperament differed from everyone else. His behavior was very spiritual and well-oriented. He was also one of my best friends. Whenever he came to school, he always brought delicious bread and cheese. Aḥmad never ate alone! He always invited us to join him and our friends, and I would do so!

Aḥmad's behavior and demeanor were examples for all of us. He was my closest and best friend during our teenage years. We played together, went to school, walked, and so on. I was in the same class as Aḥmad ʿAlī from elementary to high school. My best memories are from those days.

Sometimes, he would say, "Let us recite the short chapters of the Noble Qur'ān on our way to school." During recess, I saw him holding some papers and engrossed in reading. Once, I asked him, "What are those papers?" He said, "These are sheets containing the names of God. The divine names of God are written on these papers."

As we grew older, the spiritual gap between us widened. He kept ascending and growing with each step while I... [did not].

Aḥmad paid the most attention to prayer. He never abandoned praying on time, even when busy or occupied with work.

I remember the teacher saying, "You have an exam." The school supervisor came to the front of the class and said, "Contrary to usual practice, the exam will be held outside class hours. Be prepared for the exam tomorrow after the third bell rings."

We entered the courtyard, and they said, "The exam will start in a few minutes." The call to prayer echoed from the local mosque. Aḥmad slowly moved towards the school prayer room. I followed after him and said, "Aḥmad, come back! The teacher is very strict. If you are late, he will not let you take the exam..." Aḥmad's prayers were lengthy; he also obliged himself to recite the tasbīḥ (prayer beads) carefully. But no matter what I said, it was of no use.

Aḥmad went to the prayer room and began his prayers. At the same time, they lined us up, and we entered our classroom. The supervisor said, "Be quiet until the teacher brings the exam questions."

I kept looking towards the prayer room, worried about Aḥmad. It was a shame an excellent student like him was deprived of the exam. We sat silently in the classroom for twenty minutes. Neither the teacher, nor the supervisor, nor Aḥmad showed up! The other kids were busy whispering and chit-chatting with each other when suddenly the door opened. The teacher entered with the exam papers.

We all stood up. The teacher exclaimed angrily, "It took forever for these papers to be ready because of this copying machine!" Then he called on one of the students and said, "Get up and pass these papers around." As the teacher spoke, the door creaked open again, and Aḥmad appeared in the doorway.

Our teacher had a moral code not to let anyone enter the class after him. I anxiously waited to see his reaction. The teacher, still focused on the class, said, "Nayrī, go and take your seat!" Aḥmad sat down and began answering the exam questions. I stared at him in shock.

Aḥmad answered the questions like the rest of us. The difference between him and me was that Aḥmad had performed his prayers on time, and I... [had not].

I pondered deeply on his actions. This incident was nothing but the result of Aḥmad's sincere deeds.

Transformation

Dr. Muḥsin Nūrī

Aḥmad was similar to others. He led a simple and ordinary life like everyone else. In social gatherings, he was just like everyone else. He laughed with others and spoke like them. Aḥmad was never considered superior to them, while we all knew he was higher than the rest.

Even from middle school, when we became involved in the revolutionary movement, I sensed that I lagged far behind Aḥmad. I felt like Aḥmad knew God ﷻ and served Him differently.

While we prayed to fulfill our obligation, I saw Aḥmad gain pleasure from his prayers and munājāt (whispered prayers) with God ﷻ. Perhaps for a scholar and a mystic, enjoying prayer is an ordinary thing, but for a twelve-year-old boy, it was unusual. I tried to spend more time with him to see what he was doing. However, his behavior was very ordinary. He talked and laughed like everyone else. I only saw that when someone trailed down the wrong path, he would quietly and subtly correct them privately. He did not abandon enjoining good and forbidding evil. He only got angry when he saw someone backbiting and talking behind others' backs.

Under those circumstances, he did not care about age. He would approach the individual and firmly ask them to stop backbiting. At that time, I was Aḥmad's closest friend. We shared secrets. One day, I asked him, "Aḥmad, we have been together since childhood. But I have a question for you! I do not know why you have grown spiritually in recent years, but I... [have not]."

He smiled and tried to change the subject, but I repeated my question, "There must be a reason for it; you have to tell me!" After much insistence, he finally raised his head and said, "Can you handle it?"

Surprised, I asked, "Handle what!?" He replied, "Sit down, and I will tell you." He took a deep breath and said, "One day, we went to Damāvand with the local boys and the guys from the mosque. You were not with me on that trip. While the others were busy playing and having fun, one of the elders said, 'Aḥmad, go and fill that kettle with water and bring it here so we can make tea.'"

"Then he pointed in a direction and said, 'There is a river there. Go there and fetch water,' and I set off. The path was long, but I could hear the sound of water as I got closer. A cool breeze came from the direction of the river towards me. I approached the riverbank, passing through bushes and shrubbery.

"The moment my eyes fell on the river, I dropped my head and sat there. My body started shaking. I did not know what to do.

"I hid behind the trees there. No one could see me from where I was. The trees and bushes provided good cover for me."

With eyes widened in astonishment, I waited for Aḥmad to continue his story. "Why was he so frightened?" I thought.

Aḥmad continued, "I could have easily committed a major sin. Girls were swimming behind those trees and beside the river.

"I called upon God and said, 'Oh God, help me. God, right now, Shayṭān is tempting me intensely to look. Nobody will notice it, either. But God, I will refrain from this sin for Your sake.'

"I picked up the empty kettle and quickly moved away from there. Then, I fetched water from another place and returned to the group. My mosque friends were still busy playing, so I got busy making a fire. I collected some firewood and struggled to prepare the fire. Much smoke got into my eyes. Tears were continuously flowing from my eyes.

"I remembered that Ḥajj Āghā had told me, 'Anyone who sheds tears for God, God will love him very much. So, as tears fell from my eyes, I said to myself, 'From now on, I will cry for God.'

"I felt deeply transformed. I was still shaken by the difficult test that I had faced by the riverside. Tears streaming down my face, I prayed fervently to God, saying, 'Ya Allāh, Ya Allāh...'

"Suddenly, I heard a majestic voice echoing from all around me. Unconsciously, I stood up and looked around in astonishment. The voice reverberated from every rock and hill in the desert. It echoed from all the trees and mountains!

"They were all saying,

سبوح قدوس ربنا ورب الملائكة والروح

Subūḥun Quddūs Rabbunā
wa Rabbu al-Malā'ikah wa al-Rūḥ

Glory be to our Lord, the Holy,
the Lord of the Angels and the Spirit

"As I heard this voice, I gazed around in disbelief. I realized that none of the children playing had heard anything!

"That evening, trembling with fear, I walked around. I felt like I could hear the particles of the universe resonating with this voice!"

Aḥmad fell silent for a moment. Then, in a calm voice, he continued, 'Since that moment, little by little, doors from the higher realms have opened up to me!'

After saying this, Aḥmad stood up to leave. Then, he turned back and said, 'Muḥsin, I did not tell you this to boast about myself. I told you so you know what station a human being can acquire with God by abstaining from sin."

Then he said, "As long as I live, do not speak about this incident to anyone."

Lifestyle

Aḥmad Āghā became a perfect example of Islāmic morality and behavior in his teenage years. Everything he did was undoubtedly by Islāmic teachings. One of his special traits was his extraordinary respect for his parents. For example, whenever his mother entered the room, he stood up out of respect for her.

This respect extended to the point where Aḥmad felt upset when he came to the mosque. Surprised, I asked him why he was upset. He replied, "Every time my mother enters my room, I stand up. Today, my mother asked me, 'Why do you do this? I get annoyed with all this respect you show me.'"

Aḥmad valued maintaining close family ties. When we flip through the pages of his diary, we encounter the life of an ordinary person. For example, at one point, he narrates, "I went to my aunt's house today and got to chat with them. Then I came home and went to get some bread. Afterward,

I rested briefly, headed to the mosque, returned, and got busy studying."

It was the same way in the mosque. On the surface, his life seemed ordinary.

Aḥmad learned his manners from his teacher, Āyatullāh Ḥajj Āghā Ḥaqq-Shinās. He always took the lead in greeting others, even young children. We never saw Aḥmad eating anything in the alleys or streets. He feared that someone in need or facing financial difficulties might see him and become upset.

Whatever pocket money Aḥmad Āghā received from his father or from working, he spent on others, especially those he knew had financial problems.

It often happened that Aḥmad would speak to us in the mosque, and people would join our group one by one. With humility, he would stand up in front of every person who joined and show them respect. God ﷻ knows how much his respect and kindness to these children affected their souls. Children who thirsted for affection were now in contact with a mentor who treated them respectfully.

I will always remember. Aḥmad never boasted about his mystical deeds; instead, he guided others through his manners and behavior by the teachings of religion.

Aḥmad's family was relatively wealthy. His father had brought him nice sneakers from abroad, which was uncommon then. That night, Aḥmad brought the sneakers to the mosque and showed them to me.

He knew my family was not financially well-off, so he insisted I take the sneakers, saying, "I have another one."

He acted upon all mustaḥabb (recommended acts) he heard about. For example, I remember one time he performed a challāh (forty-day ritual) sweeping the doorstep of his house. He was not attached to having a bed or specific bedding arrangements at home. Despite having everything he needed at home, he had a blanket and easily slept on the floor.

Aḥmad worked in a tea shop owned by one of his relatives. He did not need the money, but he knew that the Ahl al-Bayt عليهم السلام considered free time the greatest danger to young people. Aḥmad's job in the tea shop was packaging tea. Tea was then mixed and sold in red and yellow packages. He received his wages at the end of the week. When he received his wages, he calculated the religious tax (khums) on his earnings and gave the share of the Sayyids (descendants of the Prophet Muḥammad ﷺ) to one of the righteous Sayyids. He indirectly gave the share of the Imām عجل الله تعالى فرجه الشريف to Ḥajj Āghā Haghashenas. However, Aḥmad's job at the tea shop did not last only a short time.

Aḥmad Āghā was an avid reader. Some of the books he studied were above the level of teenagers and young adults. He read them with the help of the seminary teachers. These books were later collected and donated to the seminary in Qom.

The Grace of the Ahl al-Bayt ﷷ

A Group of the Martyr's Friends

In a beautiful narration known as "Ḥadīth-e Safīnah" (the Ḥadīth of the Ark), it is narrated:

"The family of the Prophet ﷺ and his household are like the Ark of Nūḥ (Noah). Whoever boards it will be saved, and whoever separates from it will drown."

I sat in the mosque beside Aḥmad, discussing love and tawassul (intercession) to the Ahl al-Bayt ﷷ. Aḥmad Āghā said, "What I am about to say is not to boast or anything of the sort. I want to emphasize the importance of connecting and seeking intercession through the Ahl al-Bayt."

He continued, "Once, I saw Paradise with all its beauty in dreams. You cannot imagine how magnificent it was. I did not want to stay here longer, so I hurried towards Paradise."

Aḥmad continued, "But the further I went, the narrower and narrower my path became! It was as thin as a hair. I felt like I was about to fall from the height at any moment."

"It was then that I realized this must be the Ṣirāt (the bridge to Paradise), the one they say is thinner than a hair and sharper than a sword."

I was at a loss about what to do! I had no way forward or backward. Suddenly, it occurred to me that God has blessed us, the Shīʿa, with the Ahl al-Bayt. So I called out to the Holy Infallibles loudly.

"Suddenly, I felt their hands taking mine and saving me from that perilous situation."

He added, "You see, after tawakkul (trusting in God), we need to seek tawassul (intercession) through the Ahl al-Bayt in all stages of life. Finding this world's true Ṣirāt (path) would be impossible without their grace."

Then I referred to the luminous ḥadīth from Imām al-Mahdī, which states, "We are fully aware of all the events and occurrences that befall you, and nothing regarding your affairs is hidden from us. Despite the mistakes and sins that the righteous servants of God try to conceal from us, we are aware of them. If it were not for our grace and attention, the calamities and adversities of your life would overwhelm you, and your enemies would destroy you."

***

I knew Aḥmad from the days before the revolution and our Qur'ān sessions in the mosque. Since adolescence, he played with his peers, talked, laughed, and so on.

But I cannot recall seeing a makrūh (disliked) act from him, let alone any major sin. His life continued like that of an ordinary person, but if you spent some time with him, you would realize that he was one of the sincere servants of God ﷻ.

Once, a basīj (mobilization) rally lasted until three in the morning. Afterward, Aḥmad quietly went to the mosque's prayer hall and began the night prayer.

I watched him from a distance. His demeanor had changed. It seemed as if God ﷻ stood before him, and he, like a weak servant, was engrossed in conversing with the Lord. His loving worship seemed very strange. We saw what we heard about the prayers of grand personalities embodied in Aḥmad Āghā.

The knot of his prayer became lengthy and puzzled me so much that I had to ask him about it.

After the prayer ended, I asked him, "Aḥmad Āghā, did something happen during your qunūt?"

Aḥmad always pondered deeply before responding. After contemplating, he said, "No, nothing special happened." He wanted to change the subject, but I insisted so much that he was forced to tell me. "I was performing qunūt when it suddenly felt like I had stepped out of the mosque's atmosphere. You would not believe it! I witnessed everything, all that they say about the beauty of Paradise and the horrors of hell. I saw all the Prophets standing next to each other..."

***

We got into the backseat of a fast-moving car. The vehicle had no doors at the back, and one or two inside individuals would fall out with each turn!

The road was rough, and the car was speeding. Suddenly, I looked around and realized I was the only one left in the back of the car! As the next turn approached, it went so fast that my hand separated, and...

I was close to falling out of the car, but at that very moment, I shouted, "Ya Ṣāḥib al-Zamān عجّل الله تعالى فرجه الشريف!"

Immediately, someone grabbed my hand and did not let me fall to the ground. I was able to navigate through those neck-breaking turns safely.

At that moment, I woke up from the dream. I understood that we must hold on to the Imām of our time عجّل الله تعالى فرجه الشريف even in difficult circumstances. Otherwise, the storms of life will surely destroy us. Aḥmad shared this story with the children at the mosque.

Ascension (Miʿrāj)

Ustādh Muḥammad Shāhī

In the first year of the 60s (1982 A.D.), the country's situation was complicated due to war and internal and external enemies. Aḥmad Āghā and I were neighborhood friends. My house was south of the Amīn al-Dawlah Mosque, and Aḥmad's was north of the mosque.

I was four years younger than him, but his personality greatly influenced me. Aḥmad Āghā placed great importance on performing his prayers on time, to the extent that he would abandon all tasks during prayer time. I will never forget those days. During prayers, Aḥmad seemed to see no one but the Lord. He was detached from the world and fervently engaged in munājāt (whispered supplication) to God ﷻ.

His character had an impact on all the youth around him. Our friends also became committed to performing their prayers on time. Of course, this was also influenced by the teachings of scholars like Ḥajj Āghā Ḥaqq-Shinās. He shared many stories and traditions about the virtues of performing the prayers on time and with the presence of heart.

We lived at the intersection of Māwlavi and Sayyid Ismāʿīl in Tehrān. The neighborhood conditions greatly influenced the boys, encouraging an atmosphere of disorderly and gang-like behavior, but the strange thing was that the boys considered Aḥmad their teacher.

After prayers, we would gather inside the mosque at night, and Aḥmad would teach us the Islāmic rulings. Then, he would discuss and advise us, and we would part ways. Aḥmad Āghā was an exemplary teacher and a guide on the path of God ﷻ. We had seen in the mosque many times that Āyatullāh Ḥaqq-Shinās would call and privately specially advise him.

I had never seen Aḥmad Āghā advising anyone in the presence of others. Instead, he would write small notes and jot down our moral shortcomings. Then, he would privately hand them over to his students.

With each passing day, Aḥmad Āghā's spiritual state would change. No matter how much we progressed, his prayers became more meaningful. It reached a point where he tried to distance himself from others during prayer!

A small corner at the back of Masjid Amīn al-Dawlah was far from the worshippers' view. Only one person could pray there. Aḥmad Āghā often went there and joined the congregation.

Once, when Aḥmad Āghā started praying, I went to him and prayed beside him. Minutes later, I regretted my action! After starting the prayer, Aḥmad Āghā underwent a profound transformation. His body trembled. It was as if a weak servant had been placed before a Majestic King. Aḥmad Āghā's prayer was such that we heard it from religious scholars. He was humble in front of the Almighty. If he was able to achieve a higher level of spiritual perfection in life, it was because of this humility in the presence of God ﷻ.

In our traditions, prayer is introduced as the miʿrāj (ascension) of the believer. When I look at my prayers, I do not see any signs of ascension to the court of God ﷻ. But my whole-hearted belief, and that of Aḥmad Āghā's students, was that all his prayers, especially in the last few years of his life, displayed signs of spiritual ascension! That is, each prayer of Aḥmad Āghā elevated him closer to his Lord.

However, Aḥmad Āghā was very modest and never spoke of his inner spiritual state. But if anyone paid close attention, they would surely notice the inner luminosity. The prayer of the believer's ascension, "I once personally heard him mention the ḥadīth, "Prayer is the [point of] ascension of the believer." Then he would state, "Boys, your prayers must result in ascension for you to feel the reality of servitude."

That night, I asked, "Aḥmad Āghā, did this spiritual ascension happen to you?" Usually, in such situations, he would cleverly change the subject, but that night, after my persistence, he nodded in confirmation.

***

In the journal Aḥmad Āghā left behind, strange entries can be found. He had noted down all his daily activities from 1363 AH (1984). Some pages record, "Today's prayer was exceptionally excellent" and "I experienced a very good feeling during morning prayer today." I will never forget—once Āyatullāh Ḥaqq-Shinās witnessed his prayer. Aḥmad Āghā was only a teenager at that time. He turned to Ḥajj Ḥusayn Nayrī (Aḥmad Āghā's brother) and remarked, "I envy the state of this young man!"

All this stemmed from Aḥmad Āghā's extraordinary attention to prayer. He was truly a devout servant of God ﷻ.

***

We headed to Behesht-e-Zahrā ﷺ with Aḥmad Āghā and a few other boys from the mosque. Our usual routine was quickly passing through Behesht-e-Zahrā ﷺ to reach the congregational prayer at Masjid Amīn al-Dawlah. But we were running late that day, so we decided to pray at Behesht-e-Zahrā ﷺ instead. As we reached the beginning of the road, we encountered heavy traffic. The car came to a halt. Aḥmad checked his watch and then started talking about praying on time, but nobody responded!

Aḥmad Āghā stepped out of the car and apologized to all of us. We asked him, "Aḥmad Āghā, where are you going?"

He replied, "This traffic will not clear anytime soon, and we will not make it to the mosque to pray on time. With your permission, I will walk towards the opposite side of the road. There is a mosque where I will pray, then return to the Masjid later."

Aḥmad Āghā apologized once again and left. Wherever he was, he performed his prayers on time and with the presence of his heart. It did not matter to him if it was on the road or the street; for him, everywhere was God's ﷻ domain, and he was His devout servant.

Mobilization Forces (Basīj)

Ustādh Muḥammad Shāhī

Everyone in the neighborhood always held Aḥmad Āghā's family in high regard. Ḥamīd Riḍā, Aḥmad Āghā's elder brother, attained martyrdom in the first year of the [ʿIrāq imposed] war [on Irān][4]. It was the same year he [Aḥmad Āghā] joined the Basīj.

During his time in the Basīj at the mosque, the neighborhood youth were attracted to his morals and behavior. Whenever Aḥmad Āghā came to the mosque, a group of young people chased after him.

After a while, he was chosen as the head of the reception at the Basīj base in Amīn al-Dawlah Mosque, a mosque filled with virtuous seminarians and pious people.

Later, the responsibilities for the educational program at the mosque were also entrusted to him.

In addition to his work there, he also engaged in educational work at the Imām al-Ḥasan ﷺ Mosque.

A notable point for me was that, under normal circumstances, we lack the presence of our hearts in prayer. If we are preoccupied with worldly thoughts, we lose focus.

---

[4] The Irān-ʿIrāq War (1980-1988) was a prolonged conflict initiated by ʿIrāq, which had significant implications for Irān's military and political structures, leading to the increased prominence of organizations like the IRGC and Basīj.

If executive responsibilities are entrusted to us, then there is nothing left! Our focus during prayer is completely gone.

Aḥmad Āghā was a pious mystic whose prayers appeared as meetings with God ﷻ. Typically, such individuals either distance themselves from society or, if they engage with the community and attend mosques, refrain from getting involved in any activities to maintain their spiritual focus in prayer. We have seen many fake mystics who only know prayer, worship, and nothing else.

However, this virtuous student of Āyatullāh Ḥaqq-Shinās had learned about faith and action from his teacher.

He undertook the most difficult executive tasks in the mosque, yet his spirituality grew daily! I have seen some fake mystics engage in dhikr (remembrance of God ﷻ) and tasbīḥ (glorification of God ﷻ) when they finish their prayers.

But when Aḥmad Āghā's mystical journey concluded and his spiritual ascension ended, he joined the congregation in repeating the takbīrs (proclamations of God's ﷻ Greatness).

"Allāhu Akbar (God is the Greatest), Khumaynī Rahbar (Khumaynī is the Leader)."

He would then cup his hands in front of his face and say with the people, "Oh God, Oh God, until the revolution of the Mahdī عجل الله تعالى فرجه الشريف."

Then, he would recite the tasbīḥāt of Sayyidah Fāṭimah ﷺ with full concentration.

After praying, he performed the recommended actions, rose from his place, and returned to Basīji and educational work.

Of course, Aḥmad Āghā's likes were not rare amongst the students of the eminent Ustādh, and this was entirely due to the efforts of Ḥajj Āghā Ḥaqq-Shinās. As the pious man [Aḥmad Āghā] stated, "Āyatullāh Ḥaqq-Shinās made mysticism and wayfaring available to the lowest levels of society. He made mysticism and friendship with God a reality for the streets. There were many merchants and ordinary people who, in addition to their everyday lives, learned spiritual wayfaring from this Godly man."

***

"Always be pure and keep an eye on yourself. Conceal the faults of others. Be kind to everyone and evasive from all. As in, be with all and without need of any. Be God-wary in any clothing."

Aḥmad acted upon this statement very well. Basīj's activities were extensive due to the presence of Munāfiqīn (MEK), assassination attempts, and the conditions of the war. At that time, some Basīj forces were stationed in the mosque for a few nights to act in case of any threats.

Aḥmad, like other Basījis, stayed in the mosque during those nights. He conversed with others like an ordinary teenager. He talked, laughed, and treated everyone, even those younger than him, with good manners. But in confronting those who backbite, he did not differentiate between anyone.

Even if the person were his closest friend or someone older than him, he would respectfully ask them not to continue with that conversation.

Aḥmad Aḥmad Āghā participated in his Basīji activities like any other member. He would carry a weapon and join the nightly patrol in the Māwlavi Bāzār and surrounding areas with other Basīj units. However, the difference was that when we returned to the mosque around 3:30 a.m., and most Basījis had rested, he went inside the mosque and began his night prayers (Ṣalāt al-Layl).

In short, Aḥmad was a true Basīji, one of those Basījis whom Āyatullāh Sayyid Khumaynī[5] wanted to be resurrected with, one whom the beloved Imām ﷺ kissed on the hands and arms.

---

[5] Āyatullāh Sayyid Rūḥullāh Khumaynī was the leader of the 1979 Irān Revolution and the founder of the Islāmic Republic of Irān, whose ideology significantly shaped the nation's governance. Irān's political system is a theocratic republic where Islāmic principles guide legislation and governance, a system that emerged from the 1979 Islāmic Revolution

Cultural Instructor

Ḥusayn Hassanzadeh

He always had a gentle smile on his face. I adored this young man. He was very kind and respectful. I felt great joy whenever I saw him in the streets and alleys. Although my father always went to the mosque in those days, I would not say I liked that. Then, one day, my father took me to the mosque with him, placed my hand in the hand of that very young man, and said, "Aḥmad Āghā, I entrust my son to you!" Then he turned towards me and said, "Listen to whatever Aḥmad Āghā says. Wherever you want to go with him, you have permission, and so on." In short, he handed me over to Aḥmad Āghā. But one thing stood out as strange to me. What could my father have seen for him now to entrust me to this sixteen or seventeen-year-old young man?

Several nights passed since that incident, and I stopped going to the mosque. One night, I heard someone knocking on the house door. I went to open it—as soon as I raised my head, I saw with surprise Aḥmad Āghā standing behind the door! The second my eyes fell on him, I froze. I fell silent momentarily, thinking he had come to ask why I was not coming to the mosque.

I uttered, "Salām, Aḥmad Āghā. I swear to God that I was very busy these past few days. Forgive me." With that perpetual smile, he replied, "I did not come to ask why you are not coming to the mosque. I came to ask about your well-being. I have not seen you for a couple of days." I felt very embarrassed. What had I been thinking, and what had happened?

I said, "I am sorry. I will come tomorrow for sure." Then, another two to three days passed. During that time, whenever prayer time came by, I would be busy playing games and would skip going to the mosque.

One night, the sound of knocking came again. Even though I was engrossed in my game again, I ran out towards the door with everyone but Aḥmad Āghā in mind. When I opened the door, I died of embarrassment. He looked at me with the same smile he always bore and called my name, "Salām, Ḥusayn Āghā." He then proceeded to ask how I was. I did not say anything back. He understood I was embarrassed about not coming to the mosque and said, "Do not worry! It is not a big deal that you did not come. I am here to ask how you are." Finally, that night passed. The following night, I set out for the mosque earlier than the call to prayer, and that was the starting point of a habit. Becoming a mosque attendee became a habit.

Aḥmad Āghā attracted young people to the mosque so beautifully that it shocked us all. At that time, he was not any older than sixteen or seventeen years old, but his method of managing the cultural sphere of the mosque was amazing. At night, when prayers ended, we sat around each other for a few minutes, and the boys would recite ḥadīths or verses from the Noble Qur'ān. Aḥmad Āghā spoke less and, instead, guided us more through action.

He always mentioned the good virtues of others. For example, if someone had several faults and shortcomings but had done one good deed, he would mention that one good deed. He was always busy strengthening the positive aspects of our personalities.

Aḥmad Āghā cared more for us than a father or brother. He worked for the boys with true sincerity and love. Once, I sat next to Aḥmad Āghā in a majlis for Du'ā' al-Nudbah. Aḥmad Āghā asked me, "Can you recite the du'ā'?"

I replied, "I do not mind." He immediately placed the microphone before me, and I started reciting. I began the du'ā' with repeated errors. I made many mistakes, but after finishing the supplication, he encouraged me, saying, "Amazing! That was excellent. It was very good for your first time."

This encouragement from Aḥmad Āghā made me continue reciting, and now, with the help of God ﷻ and the favor of the Ahl-al-Bayt ﷺ, I recite in mourning ceremonies.

I will never forget the one time Aḥmad Āghā walked into the mosque during the lecture of Ḥajj Āghā Ḥaqq-Shinās. Upon noticing him, Ḥajj Āghā sent a loud Ṣalawāt, and the entire audience sent a Ṣalawāt, too. Aḥmad Āghā, becoming very shy, sat right where he was near the doorway.

Duʿāʾ al-Nudbah

He performed the morning prayer in the congregation at the mosque. After prayer, he would engage in taʿqībāt (duʿāʾ read after each prayer). He did not adopt the image of Ahl al-Dhikr (the people of remembrance) but engaged in many dhikr. Once, I went and sat next to Aḥmad Āghā. I saw him gently moving his lips. I leaned closer and realized he was busy reciting Duʿāʾ Ahad. Aḥmad Āghā always recited this supplication from memory after the morning prayer. He had a special reverence for the luminous presence of Imām al-Zamān ﷻ. He never abandoned actions that would bring a person closer to the Master of the Age ﷻ.

Not long after Basīji and cultural programs in the mosque started, Aḥmad Āghā suggested introducing a Duʿāʾ al-Nudbah program. When he announced that there would also be a breakfast program, the boys' enthusiasm increased even more! On Friday mornings, we would gather and start the du'ā' program.

He insisted that the du'ā' program be held in the main area of the mosque so that people could participate. He sincerely worked from the early morning, preparing breakfast and tea. Sometimes, after the supplication ended, Aḥmad Āghā and I would ride a motorcycle around the Cyrus Intersection. There, we would buy lentils for the boys. Thank God ﷻ that, at least for breakfast's sake, the guys got together. Aḥmad Āghā personally covered the expenses for breakfast from his pocket. He did various activities to strengthen the boys' spirituality and devotion to the Imām of the Age عجل الله تعالى فرجه الشريف.

In this very Du'ā' al-Nudbah program, he nūrtured many for the future and placed their hands in the hands of their Master.

Friday Prayer

A Number of the Martyr's Students

Aḥmad Āghā centered the mosque's cultural and educational activities around Ahl al-Bayt ﷺ and achieved many great results. Of course, Aḥmad Āghā's collective efforts for the boys were wider than just Du'ā' al-Nudbah. On some Friday nights, he took everyone to the Mahdīyah of Tehrān for Du'ā' Kumayl. On the way back, he would buy sandwiches for the boys, bringing them much joy.

But Aḥmad was very upset that the guys from the Basīj and the mosque were not interested in understanding the correct teachings of religion. He made great efforts to elevate the children's level of knowledge and belief.

He had spoken to the Basīj mosque authorities several times, advising them to focus more on raising the children's intellectual level than military activities. For this purpose, he took matters into his own hands. He attended the akhlāq (ethics) lessons of grand scholars in Tehrān with the boys. He went with them on religious occasions to the mosque of Ḥajj Āghā Javdan. He had special respect for this divine scholar. He took the mosque's educational officials to the Ḥajj Āghā Mujtabā Tihrānī gatherings.

When he felt the lectures were too heavy for everyone, he changed them and went to other scholars.

Among the other activities that repeated nearly every week was the ziyārah program of Ḥaḍrat 'Abd al-'Aẓīm Ḥasanī. We went to ziyārah with the guys and sat in front of the shrine, and upon Aḥmad Āghā's suggestion, Āghā Muḥammadī Shāhī recited eulogies for us.

Along with the boys, we headed to the service of the late Āyatullāh Nāṣir Ṣarrafhā (Qarati) in the local mosque of the Chāl neighborhood. He was the father of two martyrs and one of the pillars of his time. He gave very good ethical advice to scholars and students.

He once told us, "Āghā! Do not abandon Friday prayers. You do not know how many blessings attending Friday prayers bring a person, especially when the weather is very cold or hot (when fewer people show up)!" The other students of Aḥmad Āghā and I became overjoyed with his words since, for as long as we can remember, we had attended Friday prayers with Aḥmad Āghā.

Aḥmad Āghā got us all into Friday prayers. He gathered everyone with difficulty, and then we would proceed to the

Māwlavi intersection, take a bus or van, and finally reach Friday prayers after much difficulty.

The guys had a habit of messing around, but Aḥmad Āghā continued to familiarize them with religious knowledge with indescribable patience and tolerance.

One of the guys would say, "I got into the habit of attending Friday prayers from the time of Aḥmad Āghā. After Aḥmad Āghā's martyrdom, I also tried not to miss my Friday prayers. Then, once in a dream, I saw myself standing in a street. Aḥmad Āghā came towards me from a distance and hugged me. It was a very beautiful feeling. I was seeing Aḥmad Āghā after many years. After greeting each other, I looked at the street sign, 'Quds Street.' I realized this is where the Friday prayer is held.

I woke up then and understood that Aḥmad Āghā had given me special treatment because of my consistent presence in the Friday prayers.

Field Trip

The Muḥammad Shāhī Brothers

Some days, Aḥmad Āghā advised me, "Do not forget Ḥajj Āghā's lecture tonight!" He would say, "Kamāl, come tonight; there is important news!" During the nights he encouraged me to attend, the atmosphere of Āyatullāh Ḥaqq-Shinās's lecture was transforming.

The lectures on those nights had a strange spiritual aura. I do not know what Aḥmad Āghā saw that caused him to speak of them like he did.

We had been friends since we were young. We used to play football together when we were children. But after Aḥmad Āghā became active in the mosque, I never saw him playing football again. Once, I saw him playing with a couple of boys.

His football skills were incredible. He dribbled past defenders effortlessly, and no one could take the ball from him. He was very good at the game.

He dribbled past everyone, but as he reached the opponent's goal, he would pass the ball to one of the youngsters to score!

Aḥmad would join the team of people not affiliated with the mosque or the Basīj.

After the game, I asked him, "Aḥmad, what are you doing with these guys?" He said, "They did not have enough players, so they asked me to play, and I accepted." Then he continued, "Football is a great means to attract the boys towards the mosque."

Following the game, a number of the boys from the mosque told me, "We did not know Aḥmad Āghā could play so well!" I replied, "I had seen his skills before. I knew he played well."

When his brother was martyred, Aḥmad Āghā was one of the youth players of Esteghlāl Football Club. I told them, "Realize the value of this coach of yours. Aḥmad Āghā is a coach in all things."

***

Another cultural program that Aḥmad Āghā paid much attention to was field trips. Once, he arranged a trip to

Mashhad for the mosque boys, and at that time, the facilities were not like they are today.

The boys messed around a lot, too. During this trip, he was troubled, but later, we heard him say, "It was a very blessed ziyārah." I said, "For you, it was nothing but trouble and frustration." However, Aḥmad Āghā only spoke of the trip's blessings and Imām 'Alī al-Riḍā's ziyārah 🕌.

We did not know what Aḥmad had seen on this trip. Why did he speak of it so favorably? Later, we would learn from his journal about memories of a very strange incident relating to this trip that read, "While I was in the Holy Shrine, I got very upset seeing the poor state of ḥijāb [of the women], among other things. Therefore, I decided not to enter the shrine for fear of looking at non-maḥram. Then, Āghā [Imām Riḍā 🕌] instructed me to enter the shrine."

On other pages, he had noted about the same trip, "On Tuesday, November 4, I was in the Holy Shrine. From nine-thirty to eleven o'clock, there was a very peaceful atmosphere. Alḥamdulilāh." Aḥmad Āghā also planned ziyārah programs for the boys to the martyrs' graves in Behesht-e-Zahrā 🕌. We traveled to Behesht-e-Zahrā 🕌 almost every week with difficulty and enjoyed a very good and spiritual ziyārah.

The Guys of the Mosque

A Group of the Martyr's Students

"I have the utmost certainty that God has shown such kindness to Aḥmad Āghā because of his tolerance and patience amidst hardships while educating the mosque boys," one of the local elders would say. Tolerance of boys in their adolescent years, assistance of them, and not punishing them are the fundamental principles of upbringing.

Aḥmad Āghā, who started training others at sixteen, adhered to all these principles without a teacher. Additionally, it must be said that Masjid Amīn al-Dawlah's youth were different from those of other neighborhoods and mosques; they were especially keen on mischief and misbehaving.

The youth there were less inclined to spirituality and silence (a spiritual exercise) than Aḥmad Āghā was. Their ways of mischief were also strange.

In the mosque, we had a khādim (servant) named Mīrzā Abū al-Qāsim Riḍā'ī, who was very pious and simple. He had poor eyesight, and due to this, I saw Aḥmad Āghā helping him with the cleaning of the mosque many times. However, the boys bothered him as much as they could!

Once, the boys went to the mosque's storage room and saw a coffin. One exclaimed, "I will lay in the coffin and pull a cover over my body. You guys bring the mosque's khādim here and tell him the mosque warehouse has spirits and jinn!"

Thus, the boys went and brought the khādim to the storage room. They gave him a good scare, warning him to be careful on the way. Then, when Mīrzā Abū al-Qāsim arrived in front of the warehouse with the other boys, the boy lying in the coffin began shaking the cover! The first person to run away was the khādim of the mosque. In short, the guys wreaked havoc in the mosque.

On another occasion, for example, another of them took a cockroach in his palm, shook the hands of others, and released the cockroach into their hands. People constantly complained about such behaviors to Aḥmad Āghā, yet he still spoke patiently and tolerantly with the boys.

***

While Aḥmad Āghā spoke of spiritual matters, some boys would be thinking about misbehaving. For example, they would put the mosque's turbahs (prayer stones) on the heater. The turbahs got hot. Then, they looked around for someone praying, and as soon as that person went down for prostration, they switched his turbah.

For example, I remember a number of them used to bring firecrackers. When the khādim was distracted, they threw the firecrackers in the heater and quickly ran away.

Aḥmad Āghā took on their training in such an environment. He tolerated the children's mischief and, all praise to God ﷻ, achieved results. I can confidently say that many of his students reached high levels of knowledge and maʿrifah (gnosis).

One night, one of the boys went to the khādim of the mosque and said, "Can you check if my head wiping (part of wuḍūʾ (ablution)) is correct?" He wiped his hand from his head to his arms, body, and feet and continued wiping to the tip of his toes. Mīrzā, who had a pure soul, became upset and said, "What are you doing? This is incorrect!" But the boy started messing with him even more, saying, "It is fine!" Then he continued wiping his legs after his head. He continued until the khādim became very angry.

***

One of the tall boys picked up a cloak and turban. He put them on very sophisticatedly and walked into the mosque after the prayer when everyone had already left. Only us youngsters were inside the mosque. Aḥmad Āghā was not there either.

Mīrzā Abū al-Qāsim, who naturally had a very kind and pure heart, came and embraced him and asked, "Ḥajj Āghā, have you come from Qom?" To which he replied, "Yes." The poor man could not see very well. He said, "Please come and advise these youngsters a little." Then he turned to face us and said, "Come forward and learn from Ḥajj Āghā." Ḥajj Āghā, subsequently, came forward very seriously and sat down amongst the boys!

Then he said Bismillāh (In the Name of God) and began speaking. Mīrzā Abū al-Qāsim also sat before him and listened to his words. We were all dying from laughter but struggling to contain ourselves. He lectured us with a very solemn tone, repeating the words of Aḥmad Āghā. That was until the end when he suddenly changed topics and started talking about the game of marbles. Mīrzā immediately stood up from his place. With weak eyes, he stared at that person's face and said, "Wait..... it is you?"

Only God ﷻ knows how much verbal abuse Aḥmad Āghā faced from the elders after each act of mischief by the boys. Perhaps nothing in the mosque was more difficult than the condemnation Aḥmad Āghā received in the meetings of the Basīj and the mosque's trustees because of the mischief of his students. However, he faced all this criticism with a smile. He knew that the Holy Prophet ﷺ had said to Imām ʿAlī b. Abī Ṭālib (Amīr al-Muʾminīn) ؑ: "Oh ʿAlī, if even one person finds guidance through you, it is greater than that which the sun shines over." The fruits of his labor are clear now. Among those few students, many doctors, engineers, clerics, businessmen, and pious individuals were nūrtured, all of whom attribute their spiritual growth to the teachings of Aḥmad Āghā.

His students still follow the path Aḥmad Āghā paved for them. As one of his students used to say: "If the amount of effort that Aḥmad Āghā put in for us were placed on a barren tree, it would have borne fruit!"

Āyat al-Ḥaqq

In order to discuss Aḥmad Āghā properly, we must first get to know his esteemed teacher better. Under his supervision, Aḥmad Āghā was disciplined and completely obeyed his instructions.

Āyatullāh Ḥajj Mīrzā ʿAbd al-Karīm Ḥaqq-Shinās Tihrānī was born in 1920 to a religious family in Tehrān. His given name was Karīm, and his family name was Ṣafākīsh.

His father was the governor of Tehrān at that time and thus was known as "ʿAlī Khān." He had three children: Walī, Karīm, and Raḥīm.

His family home was located on Irān Street, considered one of Tehrān's prominent neighborhoods. His father passed away when his children were young, and their mother remained alive until Karīm reached the age of fifteen. He always praised his noble mother.

He would say, "My mother was illiterate, yet she read the Noble Qur'ān and the book of Mafātīḥ very well! She could even distinguish the verses of the Noble Qur'ān from other words, and she attributed this understanding to a dream of Imām 'Alī ﷺ.

She was given two loaves of bread from His Holiness ﷺ in the dream. The devil stole one, but she succeeded in preserving and eating the other. Upon waking from the dream, she could recognize and read the verses of the Noble Qur'ān!"

Upon his mother's passing, his eldest uncle, Ḥajj Mīrzā 'Alī, stepped forward and proposed, "From amongst the children, Karīm can come to our home. He can be our child." So, he spent two or three years in his uncle's house. During this time, he attended Dār al-Funūn High School. His uncle wanted him to go to the marketplace and start a business after his studies.

After all, this was the norm of the time. On the other hand, Dār al-Funūn led to university and government positions, as seen in the paths taken by their brothers, who reached positions in the Ministry of Foreign Affairs.

However, God ﷻ had ordained a different fate for Karīm. Towards the end of high school, his heart was drawn towards something else.

He succeeded in reaching Shaykh Muḥammad Ḥusayn Zāhid's presence. Although Shaykh Zāhid did not receive an extensive formal education, he excelled at applying what he had learned. He was very pious, detached from worldly affairs, and an ascetic.

He had many students, some of whom would reach lofty [spiritual] stations. With his guidance, Āghā Ḥaqq-Shinās departed his uncle's home for a chamber in the Jāmiʿ Mosque of Tehrān.

During his time in Dār al-Funūn, he mastered the latest mathematics and the French language. Consequently, he became an accountant for a merchant, telling him, "I will accept a much lower salary on the condition that I can go to the mosque to pray on time and study in the afternoons."

Āghā Ḥaqq-Shinās attended the classes of Ustādh Shaykh Muḥammad-Ḥusayn Zāhid for many years and benefited from his teachings. After some time, he began searching for a teacher higher in rank. That is when he met Āyatullāh Sayyid ʿAlī Ḥāʾirī, famously known as 'Mufassir' (interpreter).

He would say, "The night before I met him, I was shown a grand Sayyid sitting on top of a minbar (pulpit) in a dream. They told me, 'He has to take care of your upbringing.' The following day, when we arrived in the presence of Āyatullāh Mufassir, I realized that he was the same person shown to me the night before!"

Ḥajj Āghā Ḥaqq-Shinās told us on multiple occasions, "At the beginning of my studies, I was afflicted with lung issues. Sometimes, I would even cough up blood.

Tuberculosis was a dangerous disease at the time, and there was a high probability that I had it. Doctors and medication had no effect either.

One day, I gave away all that remained of my savings as ṣadaqah (charity). That night, I saw the Imām of our Time عجّل الله فرجه in my dream and requested intercession from him.

He ran his blessed hand on my chest and said, "This illness is nothing special. What is important are one's moral illnesses." Then he pointed to my heart. In short, the disease was overcome."

Then came the issue of military conscription. He was enlisted, which was not something anyone would willingly agree to during Riḍā Khān's reign[6]. For this reason, he altered his passport with the help of certain connections. "Karīm" became "ʿAbd al-Karīm," and "Ṣafākīsh" became "Ḥaqq-Shinās." His age also increased by ten, twelve, or maybe even more. Hence, his birth year is recorded as 1907 in his passport.

He used to tell us, "I went to the medical inspection site for the army to follow up on my military conscription case. As I was climbing the stairs, my heart started beating rapidly. I said, 'I am not afraid, so why is my heart beating so fast?'

"At the inspection site, the military doctors examined my heart. The examiner told the other, 'Quickly write his

---

6 Riḍā Shāh Pahlavī, founder of the Pahlavī Dynasty (1925-1979).

exemption so he can leave; this young man has at most two days left to live!'

"In any case, an exemption was granted, and I walked out. Going down the stairs, my heart rate returned to normal!"

Ḥajj Āghā was blessed to meet many scholars in Tehrān, including Āyatullāh Shahābādī and others, and later traveled to Qom.

For a time, he was the student of Āyatullāh Ḥujjat and Āyatullāh Sayyid Khumaynī. Then, when Āyatullāh Burūjirdī came to Qom, he was at his service day and night. He attended all of Āyatullāh Burūjirdī's sessions and classes of fiqh (jurisprudence) and uṣūl (principles of jurisprudence).

He took notes on everything; today, those expositions remain part of his scholarly legacy. Furthermore, he received the right of ijtihad (independent interpretation of the Shariah) from four major scholars of the time and continued his studies and research.

In 1953, Shaykh Muḥammad-Ḥusayn Zāhid, the leader of Friday prayers at Masjid Amīn-ol-doleh in Tehrān's Māwlavi Bāzār, passed away.

He wrote in his will to invite Āyatullāh Ḥaqq-Shinās to manage and lead the mosque's prayers, stating, "This individual, in terms of both knowledge and actions, is superior to me."

The elders of the neighborhood and notable mosque leaders then traveled to Qom and met with Āyatullāh Burūjirdī. They requested that he appoint Ḥajj Āghā Ḥaqq-Shināṣ to lead the Masjid.

According to those who attended this meeting, Āyatullāh Burūjirdī said, "Do not think that a simple scholar is coming to Tehrān. Rather, [it is as if] you are taking me to Tehrān with you."

Āyatullāh Ḥaqq-Shināṣ used to say to us, "My return to Tehrān was very costly. Qom was a place of progress and a path for knowledge and action, and I did not desire to come to Tehrān."

Those were very hard days for him. Seeking advice, he resorted to an old friend, his Eminence Āyatullāh Sayyid Khumaynī, who, in return, told him, "It is your duty. You must go." He asked him, "Why do you not go?" Sayyid Khumaynī replied, "I swear on my ancestors [The Holy Progeny of the Prophet ﷺ] that if they had asked for Rūḥullāh, I would have surely gone."

Whatever the case, Āghā Ḥaqq-Shināṣ came to Tehrān. The students of the late Āghā Zāhid then turned to him, and the seminary students of Tehrān went to him for their studies.

In his early youth, he was instructed that much of his spiritual wayfaring would never require letting go of congregational and on-time prayers, the night prayer, and studies and academic discussions.

At the start of the 1960s, he directed the youth of Masjid Amīn al-Dawlah, who were previously students of the late Āghā Zāhid, to the taqlīd (acting according to the verdict of a Mujtahid) of his Eminence, Āyatullāh Sayyid Khumaynī. They all obliged.

That group later served as the central hub of the Islāmist party. It was one of the first supporters and sincere companions of Sayyid Khumaynī, helping establish aspects of the coming movement and Islāmic Revolution.

Āyatullāh Ḥaqq-Shinās possessed many special qualities, and we will highlight a few prominent ones:

He was patient in the face of affliction and disease and remained so during long periods of illness.

Attending to the needs of the people and solving their problems, such that during the entire difficult phase of the [Imposed 'Irāq-Irān] war, under the bombardments and missile strikes of cities, and the desolation of Tehrān, he never left and kept attending the mosque, remaining concerned about the people. He often committed to a forty-day ritual of Ziyārat 'Āshūrā' to alleviate these calamities.

The third quality can be noted as his unique respect and honor towards his wife. He would advise others to do the same. If he knew someone was mistreating their wife, he got very angry. He used to say, "I see my perfection in the service to my wife, and I consider myself obliged to provide all that she asks for."

The fourth quality is that he was very sensitive to the sin of ghībah (backbiting). Of course, this trait is shared by all scholars of akhlāq (ethics) and those on the path of spiritual wayfaring.

He served as the headmaster of the Filsūf al-Dawlah and the Sepahsālār seminaries for some time and taught classes himself. This divine man's miracles and anecdotes are so numerous that dozens of books have been written about his virtues.

Eventually, this pious teacher passed away at the age of 88 on July 24th, 2007. After the [funeral] prayer by Āyatullāh Mahdavī Kanī, his body was taken to the holy shrine of Ḥaḍrat ʿAbd al-ʿAẓīm Ḥasanī and laid to rest there.

Āyīneh Varzān

Ḥujjat al-Islām Islāmīfar

For several years, I have traveled to the Damāvand region on behalf of the Hawza (seminary) of Qom to propagate [the religion]. I spent the months of Ramaḍān and al-Muḥarram serving the kind people of the Āyīneh Varzān village. Due to my deep respect for the martyrs, I often mention them on the pulpit. When I first arrived in this village, I realized that the believing people there had gifted fifteen martyrs to the cause of Islām and the revolution.

I always speak about the martyrs to the people and name those from such villages on the pulpit—but something was strange for me. The people became profoundly moved whenever I got to the name of Aḥmad 'Alī Nayrī. Why did they react so strongly to the memory of this martyr? Who was he?

I asked village elders about him, and they told me, "He was born here but lived in Tehrān. He only visited during the summer, and in these last few years, we have seen Aḥmad ʿAlī even less.

"You have no idea how great of a person this young man was. Any virtue that we knew of was collectively manifest in his being." Afterward, I had the opportunity to meet one of the village's seniors, who was considered one of the respected landowners and elders of Damāvand.

From his appearance, he did not seem particularly religious or devoted to the mosque or anything like that. I approached him, greeted him, and asked, "Excuse me, do you happen to have any memories of Aḥmad Nayrī?"

He looked at me and, with surprise, said, "You mean Aḥmad ʿAlī?" With joy, I confirmed. He glanced at my face, tears forming in his eyes. He repeated his name several times and began crying loudly.

I became upset. When he calmed down a bit, I posed my question again. With a lump of sadness in his throat, he said, "Neither I nor any of the locals here, or anyone else, truly knew Aḥmad. Only God knew Aḥmad. He was an angel in human form. He came for some time so our children and the locals of this region can learn about God and benefit from his being."

Tears fell from his eyes again. He continued, "When Aḥmad used to come here, he would gather all the boys. He took them to the mosque and spoke for them. He taught them the Noble Qur'ān, explained religious rulings, and played with them. Many of these boys were older than Aḥmad ʻAlī, but they all accepted him."

"Everyone loved him. Aḥmad was an expert in attracting young people to the mosque, God, and religion. The boys gathered around him in the local mosque of Āyīneh Varzān and did not leave his side for a moment. Aḥmad ʻAlī guided many of the locals here. Several traveled the way of God and religion and became martyrs after Aḥmad. May his memory live on, what a person he was. Even our elders were influenced by him. You do not know what a gem we lost.

"God knows, when he used to walk through these fields and alleys, it seemed like the walls and doors saluted him!"

The old man said all this, and tears dropped from his eyes again. When his wife saw her husband shedding tears, she asked in astonishment, "Ḥajj Āghā, what happened? I have lived with Ḥajji for fifty years now, and I have never seen him cry! What did you say to him that has caused him to cry?" In short, a similar situation occurred with other elders I visited in the village. They all remembered Aḥmad ʻAlī with fondness, regardless of their age.

Even some children knew of Aḥmad Āghā and would say, "We have heard from our father that he was a very good person..."

Two Wishes

Dr. Muḥsin Nūrī

I can say with certainty that Aḥmad Āghā had no presence of "self" in him. He had no ego that could come between him and his Beloved. This is probably why he attained some secrets of the unseen.

Sometimes, he would speak to us about certain topics for our guidance. He used to make predictions and forecasts of the future, which were very valuable to us. I was a friend of Aḥmad Āghā's. I remember one day in the last few years, he said something very striking to me. I had a secret between myself and God ﷻ that no one knew about.

Aḥmad Āghā said to me discreetly, "You have two wishes, and you have asked for two wishes from God. Whether or not God grants them to you depends on if you take good care of your actions and soul on the day of ʿĀshūrāʾ." I was shocked.

He advised me, "If you wish to observe precaution, then be vigilant of your actions the day before 'Āshūrā' and the day after 'Āshūrā', and be careful not to be negligent." He continued, "God will fulfill one of these wishes this 'Āshūrā' as long as you are vigilant of yourself."

Thank God ﷻ I was in a very good state that year. I tried very hard not to commit any sins. Then al-Muḥarram came by. During the first ten days, I increased my self-vigilance. On the day of 'Āshūrā' and the day after, I was careful not to avoid a mistake. After two to three days, I saw Aḥmad Āghā at Masjid Amīn al-Dawlah, and he squeezed my hand like usual and said, "Great work! You carried out your duties excellently. God will grant you one of your wishes." Then he asked me, "Would you like me to tell you about your wish?"

Based on my trust and love for him, I responded, "No, it is unnecessary." After a couple of days, my first wish was granted. Time passed until the eve of Arba'īn. He told me, "God desires to grant you your second wish, but He is waiting to see if you take care of your actions on the day of Arba'īn." So, I was again very heedful until the day of Arba'īn. However, on Arba'īn's day, I made a mistake.

Someone started backbiting, and I had a duty to stop this ugly act. But due to reservations, I said nothing, stood up, and even laughed a little. I quickly came to my senses and realized my wrongdoing. After that, I was very careful not to make any mistakes in my actions. I did the same the day after Arba'īn.

Following Arbaʿīn, I went to Aḥmad Āghā. I asked him about my situation, and he stated, "Unfortunately, the situation does not look good. God will not grant you that wish for the time being." Then, referring to the gathering of backbiting, he said, "You could not be vigilant when it was needed."

This spiritual grasp over his friends made Aḥmad Āghā more than just a friend to us; he was also a coach and an ethics teacher. Our circle of friends and I loved Aḥmad Āghā very much. We shared a deep affection for him. All of us, the guys of the mosque, and I loved him.

However, Aḥmad had evolved so much, traversed so many high stations, and recently gotten so close to God ﷻ that it seemed hard for him to stay in this world longer.

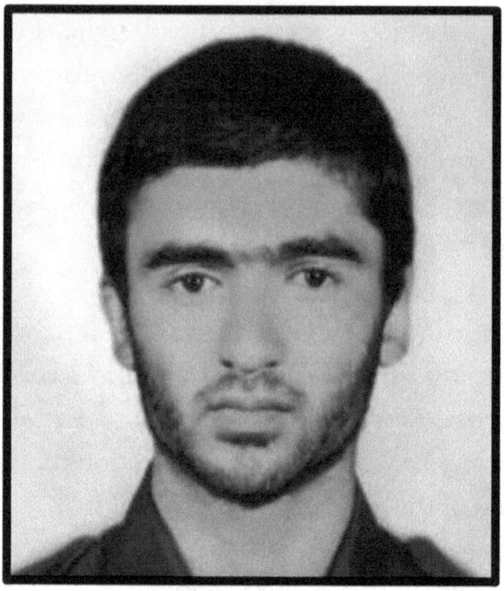

Sincerity

A Number of the Martyr's Students

A Ḥadīth al-Qudsi (a ḥadīth quoting God ﷻ) narrates, "Sincerity is a secret from among my secrets that I have entrusted to the hearts of My beloved servants."

He worked sincerely for God ﷻ. Aḥmad Āghā used to do the most arduous work in the mosque. Once, I remember that he wanted to light the heater in the mosque. Suddenly, the sound of an explosion was heard! Gas had accumulated in the heater. God ﷻ showed great mercy. A large fire from the heater's mouth burned Aḥmad Āghā's eyebrows and beard. But Aḥmad Āghā endured it patiently. He did not even let out a sigh.

Another time, while decorating the mosque for the mid-Shaʿbān celebrations, he fell from a ladder and broke his arm. But these incidents did not affect him in the slightest. He continued his work in the mosque earnestly.

He knew that Sayyidah Fāṭimah al-Zahrā' 🕮 had said in a beautiful ḥadīth, "Whoever offers his sincere worship to God 🕮 will send him that which is in his best interest."

I had heard Aḥmad Āghā was busy scripting a copy of the Noble Qur'ān. He once wrote the entire Qur'ān and then gifted it to one of his friends.

Now, he had started to write one for a second time. But this time, he did not still need to finish it! I asked him, "Well, since you have started already, why don't you finish it and give it to me?" He responded, "No, at first my intentions were sincere, but now I feel that I lack the necessary sincerity for this work."

According to his mother, Aḥmad had no desires or whims. We never saw him say he liked a certain food or wanted something. He was not like that. His life was simple and free of contamination [from the carnal self]. He never chased after fashion, stylish clothes, etc.

Of course, be correct; Aḥmad Āghā was always presentable. A simple and clean coat, short hair and beard, and a joyful and uniquely calm face that drew a person closer to God 🕮 were among the characteristics derived from the sincerity of Aḥmad Āghā.

He often remarked to his students,

"That person's facial nūr (light) has decreased!"

"So and so, you are not accompanied by good friends!"

Conversely, he had the same attitude towards the good deeds of others. He mentioned these things with sincerity.

Aḥmad Āghā made sure to mention these things for those seeking spiritual growth. He spoke to them with sincerity and tried to elevate their spirituality higher.

Understanding

Friends of the Martyr

I have often wondered what the way towards salvation and felicity is. Is it in distancing from people or being with them? Is it possible to become a friend of God ﷻ and simultaneously be in the story of life? How can contradicting acts be done together? To socialize with people, study, work, laugh and cry with friends, taste the bitterness and sweetness of time, and simultaneously experience ascension in prayers.

I have often asked myself, "Has the path to the station of servitude reached its end? Are the likes of Aḥmad Āghā unattainable role models?" and a hundred other questions. But looking at Aḥmad Āghā's daily life, we see that the way to reach God ﷻ, the ones near Him (Qurb Ilāhī), and those amongst His friends (Awliyā' al-Ḥaqq) is created in the context of life's journey. Under these circumstances, the entire system of existence becomes the cradle of human growth.

It should be noted that the important difference between Aḥmad Āghā and others stemmed from his 'understanding' of the meaning of existence. In this manner, his actions, however small, were spiritual and of immeasurable value. He was a rational human being, and this was a prominent trait in the students of His Eminence, Āyatullāh Ḥaqq-Shinās.

The significance of this attribute lies in the fact that in our era, false and pseudo-mysticism has become a threat to the lives of God's ﷻ true lovers. Unfortunately, we witness many who, neglecting the luminous path of reason, embark on non-Qur'ānic, irrational, and self-made paths to mysticism. They delude themselves into thinking that religiosity and friendship with God ﷻ necessitate abandoning human duties and obligations, falling into the false notion that neglecting worldly responsibilities is synonymous with devotion to God ﷻ. These are individuals who, in their delusion, lead themselves and their simple-minded followers towards destruction.

However, Aḥmad Āghā, as a wise mystic, attended to all the responsibilities of life. He engaged in studies, work, sports, cleanliness, social interactions, political and social analysis, and more. These actions made him an exemplary role model.

The neighborhood boys still vividly remember his work and actions. They remember playing football with him or how he poured tea for people in the mosque's courtyard.

Aḥmad Āghā's correct understanding of life and servitude elevated him to the pinnacle of devotion. At a young age, he dealt with the events of the world like an experienced adult, perceiving the truth behind his actions.

One time, we went to the village of Āyīneh Varzān with him. After some fun and games, we sat down next to each other. A bee was buzzing around my face. I tried to swat it away from me with anger and frustration. But Aḥmad Āghā, sitting beside me, paid no attention to the bee and, instead, watched my actions. Then he smiled and said, "Have certainty!" Seeing my wonder, he continued, "Be certain that no [dangerous] creature of God would harm a believer."

Jamāl

My brother Jamāl was one of Aḥmad Āghā's close friends. Aḥmad Āghā's behavior was a big influence on him. They always attended the Ustādh Ḥaqq-Shinās lessons together. Jamāl's morals and behavior were very similar to Aḥmad Āghā's. At that time, our family's circumstances were entirely different from theirs. While Jamāl was in elementary school, he worked at a shop.

Our father was a simple worker with several heads of families. He collected and gave whatever Jamāl earned to our father or mother for the household expenses. Although the conditions of our house were nothing to brag about from a financial standpoint, I would see Jamāl worrying about other people's problems often and trying to solve them. Another of his characteristics was his heartfelt devotion and incredible love for his masters, Qamar Banī Hāshim (ʿAbbās b. ʿAlī) and the Imām of the Time عجل الله تعالى فرجه الشريف.

Jamāl left for the front lines with the outbreak of the [imposed Irān-ʿIrāq] war. In 1983, he took leave after a long time and bid farewell to all his friends. Jamāl and some friends would always say they wish to remain anonymous! Their wish was fulfilled during Operation Valfajr 4 in the country's western highlands. For some time, we did not receive any news from them.

My mother loved Jamāl dearly and was more anxious than any of us. Then, one day, good news arrived! One of Jamāl's friends had come to the neighborhood. He told us, "I am sure Jamāl is alive. He is wounded and will return soon!"

I was so happy that I did not know what to do. I ran to the mosque. In times of joy and distress, Aḥmad Āghā was my steadfast rock. I was with him day and night.

I entered the Basīj office with joy. Aḥmad Āghā was busy making a placard with the inscription, "The ascension of Martyr Jamāl Muḥammad Shāhī..." when I said, "Do not write, Aḥmad Āghā!"

"Good news, good news!" I could not even form the words fully due to my excitement. "Aḥmad Āghā, one of Jamāl's friends, said that Jamāl was alive. He saw Jamāl wounded and taken to the hospital..." I stared into Aḥmad Āghā's eyes. He did not become happy at all! He lowered his head and continued writing. I said, "Aḥmad Āghā, stop writing. Did you not hear me? Jamāl is alive. If my mother sees this placard, she will collapse."

He lifted his head and said, "I saw your Jamāl. He was in paradise. He became a martyr two months ago during the operation!" It felt like cold water had been poured over me. Waves of shock came over me. I trusted Aḥmad Āghā's words. I looked at him with a sense of bewilderment. All the memories of my brother Jamāl flashed before my eyes. I swallowed hard and asked, "Did my brother say anything else?"

He looked up again and replied, "Yes. He asked me to pray two months of qaḍā' (missed) prayers for him; I have been doing it for some time now." After that, we were certain that Jamāl had become a martyr. A few days later, we discovered that the news of his injury also turned out to be a mistake. Jamāl's memorial service was held in the mosque. Aḥmad Āghā gathered all the boys and participated in the ceremony. He also sat in the mosque very politely.

Much later, when I asked him, he told me, "Our master, the Imām of the Time ﷻ, was present at Shahīd Jamāl's funeral. For this reason, I insisted that all the boys attend."

Jamāl joined the ranks of the anonymous martyrs, and his body never returned. Later, a friend of Jamāl who resided in Qom called and said, "I saw Jamāl in my dream, and he told me, 'We have returned with the anonymous martyrs and are present near the Jamkarān Mosque, on top of Khaḍir Mountain!'"

After a long time, I heard from Aḥmad Āghā that Āyatullāh Ḥaqq-Shinās, regarding the importance of prayer, had said, "My dear brother, the importance of prayer is such that even that martyr comes and tells his friend to perform two months of prayers for him. Even a martyr does not want the burden of Ḥaqq Allāh (the right of God ﷻ) on his shoulders."

Missing

A Friend of the Martyr and Ustādh Muḥammad Shāhī

We were in the Basīji base of the mosque. After finishing and reviewing my work, I wanted to return home. As usual, I said goodbye to the guys. when I was about to leave, Aḥmad Āghā said, "Do you want me to give you a ride on my motorcycle?" I replied, "No, my house is close by. I will walk through Māwlavi Bāzār myself."

He looked at me again and said, "What if a dog follows and bothers you?" I replied, "No way, what dog? I walk this way every night." He repeated, "Let me take you." But I did not allow it and said, "Thank you for your kindness." Then, I left the mosque.

I passed through the mosque's alley and entered Māwlavi Bāzār. Suddenly, I saw seven or eight big, black dogs ahead of me in the bāzār! What should I do? Where did they come from? Should I go forward or turn back?

In short, I shouted for the mosque boys. Only then did I remember Aḥmad Āghā's words. Did he know those dogs would block my way?

***

He had several sons. One of them went to the war front. Sometime later, his son went missing during an operation. Many said that his son was martyred during the operation.

Some even said that they had seen the body of this martyr. Everyone from the neighborhood knew him as the father of a martyr.

This father was very hardworking but was not a regular attendee of the mosque or congregational prayers. He had another characteristic: his special admiration for Aḥmad Āghā. Recently, when Aḥmad Āghā had become very spiritual, talk of the same man's son came up.

Quickly and firmly, Aḥmad Āghā said, "His son has not been martyred; he is currently a prisoner in an ʿIrāqi prison." Then he continued, "A day will come when his son will return."

I was really happy. I went to that father and told him, "Do you have confidence in Aḥmad Āghā?" He said, "Yes, Aḥmad Āghā is the best and purest youth in this neighborhood." With delight, I told him, "Aḥmad says your son is alive. He is currently a prisoner in an ʿIrāqi prison and will return."

He became very happy and asked, "Did you hear this directly from Aḥmad Āghā?" I replied, "Yes, he was talking about your son in the mosque just a moment ago." He accompanied me to the mosque. Then he sat next to Aḥmad Āghā and started speaking to him. Just hearing from Aḥmad Āghā was enough for this simple-hearted old man. He did not go searching for evidence and documents. He shed tears and thanked God ﷻ. After that conversation, the family repeatedly inquired with the Red Cross, but they received no news.

Some considered this father naive for trusting the words of a young man and claiming that his son was alive. But this father had complete trust in Aḥmad Āghā's words. During that time, he also had a dream that confirmed Aḥmad Āghā's words.

From that day on, this father never missed a congregational prayer. He always came to the mosque and found greater respect and appreciation for the boys of the mosque, especially Aḥmad Āghā. The truth of Aḥmad Āghā's words came to fruition five years later. In August of 1990, the prisoners of war were exchanged between Irān and ʿIrāq.

Then, it was announced that several missing Irānians who had been in Ṣaddām Ḥusayn's secret camps had been released.

Masjid Amīn al-Dawlah and the surrounding neighborhood were illuminated with lights. The freed prisoner of war, Abū al-Faḍl Mīrzā'ī, whom nobody was sure was alive until his release, returned home. But that day, Aḥmad Āghā was no longer among us.

Mystical

I once asked Aḥmad Āghā, "How are you aware of such matters? The issue of Jamāl's martyrdom, Abū al-Faḍl being alive, and a few other things I have seen from you."

As usual, Aḥmad Āghā spoke about self-vigilance and self-monitoring. He said, "Try not to sin to the best of your ability. Be vigilant of your actions as much as you can. You will see the world at your service when you have done so."

Then he looked at me and continued, "You have to [spiritually] elevate to witness certain things! You have to reach a higher status so I can tell you some things!"

Then he said something that I still find difficult to comprehend. He said, "God has shown me the lives of individuals! God has shown me the blessings that are bestowed upon individuals!

"Some people come to Ḥajj Āghā Ḥaqq-Shinās's classes on Friday nights. They are very grand individuals, able to perceive the innermost truths of others. So be careful with your actions."

***

Most of what we heard from Aḥmad Āghā was about self-improvement. Once, while we were sitting together with a number of the guys, Aḥmad Āghā said, "Guys, let us think about our actions a little."

Then he stated, "Everyone, someone from amongst us, will become a martyr. Let us engage in self-improvement so martyrdom becomes our destiny as well." He continued, "Guys, try to be free from sin for at least three days. Divine favors will surely reach you if you engage in contemplation and accountability of your actions for three days."

The guys asked Aḥmad Āghā, "What can we do to get closer to God?" Aḥmad Āghā replied, "Refrain from sin for forty days. Rest assured that your ears and eyes will be opened." This refers to the famous ḥadīth: "Whoever commits his actions sincerely for God for forty days, God will spur springs of wisdom in his tongue."

***

For certain reasons, Aḥmad Āghā showed me more kindness. Our family was very big, and we lived in a small house. My brother had also been martyred, so he paid special attention to my training. He always conveyed some teachings to the other kids through me.

He once told me, "Tell our mosque friends not to lie. When falsehood comes out of someone's mouth, it spreads a stench of filth in the air that I cannot bear!"

Mystical Deeds

The Martyr's Friends

Āyatullāh Jawādī Āmulī (may God ﷻ protect him) states [7]: "If worship is accompanied by contemplation that helps the soul recognize the truth, it places man entirely on the path of truth and leads to his salvation.

In worship, the body becomes completely obedient to the soul, and if the human soul realizes the truth through contemplation in this state, he will be placed entirely on the path of truth.

Otherwise, man will achieve nothing but wickedness. As stated in a narration,

---

[7] Āmulī, Āyatullāh 'Abd Allāh Jawādī, *'Amal 'Irfānī dar Parto 'Ilm wa Ḥayānī*, p. 39.

'Be aware of the worship that is void of contemplation, because there is no good in it.'[8]

"The mystic does everything on the orders of Huwa al-Awwal (He (who is) is the First) and to meet Huwa al-Ākhir (He (who is) the Last), and perceives the truth in all of its manifestations."

***

We traveled to Qom with a couple of friends. After ziyārah (pilgrimage), along with Aḥmad Āghā and friends, we went to the house of one of our companions and spent the night there. It was around midnight when Aḥmad Āghā woke up. I also woke up, but I did not get out of bed!

Aḥmad Āghā wanted to perform ablution for prayer but felt it would disturb the house owner. So, he took the Noble Qur'ān instead, sat in a corner, and read it.

He remained awake at dawn, but contrary to his usual practice, he did not perform the night prayer! I observed this behavior of his. Later, the adhān (call to prayer) was made, and our friends woke up. We performed ablution and prayed.

The next day, I spoke with him. Somehow, Aḥmad Āghā, dawn, and reciting the Noble Qur'ān came up. He said, "Due to consideration for the house owner, I could not perform ablution and pray the night prayer, but God

[8] Kulaynī, Shaykh Muḥammad b. Ya'qūb, *al-Kāfī*, Vol. 1, p. 36.

granted me a great reward and profound effects through my recitation of the Noble Qur'ān that dawn."

Aḥmad Āghā's behavior and this incident were very strange to me. That early morning, he recited the Noble Qur'ān without ablution and spoke of the favor that God ﷻ had bestowed on him! He did not want to inconvenience the homeowner for the sake of God ﷻ, and God ﷻ compensated him like this.

Aḥmad Āghā exemplified the words of his teacher, Ḥaḍrat Āyatullāh Ḥajj Āghā Mujtabā Tihrānī, who had said, "If I see that recommended actions harm my obligatory actions (or lead me to sin), I will forsake them."

Aḥmad Āghā often said, "If I feel that performing the night prayer makes me lazy in the morning for work or studies, I will forsake it."

Aḥmad Āghā believed that if an important mustaḥabb (recommended) act, such as the night prayer, prevents or disturbs the work that is obligatory upon him, the night prayer must be put aside.

Of course, he usually slept early to avoid difficulties or fatigue in performing the night prayer and daily tasks. Things became difficult for him only on those nights when he was in the Basīj and stationed.

***

We performed the morning prayer in Masjid Amīn al-Dawlah. After the prayer, I saw Aḥmad Āghā rest at the Basīj base. I had heard from him many times that sleeping between the time of fajr and sunrise is makrūh (unrecommended). So, why did Aḥmad Āghā do it?

After the Maghrib prayer, I asked him about this issue. He said, "I slept poorly last night because of the Basīj responsibilities. I feared I would slip [in my behavior] and act roughly with others during the day due to fatigue and weariness. That is why I rested."

Aḥmad Āghā's mystical actions and deeds served as a lesson for all his students and friends. Everyone benefited from the fruits of his qualities according to their capacities. He would never turn to sin. Once, writing a letter, he said, "For a believer, the weight of sin is perceived as the weight of Mount Uḥud."

He always advised against trivializing sin and being wary of doing good deeds. In a letter to one of his friends on the frontlines, he wrote, "Imām Ja'far aṣ-Ṣādiq ﷺ said,

> “Shayṭān instructs his followers to create three states in the human being so that he may be relieved: belittle sinful deeds for them, make good deeds seemingly hard and ambiguous so that they do not perform them, and create arrogance and selfishness in them.”

"My dear brothers, God forbid we become polluted in these three traps of the devil in which we are already immersed. If a true believer sins, he feels its weight on his shoulders like Mount Uḥud's. However, if a hypocrite sins, he acts like the one who fans a fly from his face."

Visiting a Friend

A Number of the Martyr's Friends

Our grand scholars believe the path to meet the Master, Authority, and Imām of the Time عجل الله تعالى فرجه الشريف is open. Some have even articulated ways and methods to their followers for meeting and communicating with the Imām عجل الله تعالى فرجه الشريف. But these same scholars have asserted, "If someone claims to have met the luminous being of Imām al-Zamān عجل الله تعالى فرجه الشريف and uses it as a means to gain fame or other worldly gains, then reject them."

In this era, numerous false claimants meet with his Eminence, and many fall for them. However, it must be said that a person who is at the pinnacle of divine servitude, a youth who is not indifferent to sin and transgression, and an individual who has renounced worldly pleasures for the sake of God ﷻ will undoubtedly ascend the ranks of perfection one after the other.

One who does not abandon Duʿāʾ ʿAḥad after congregational prayers every morning and every Friday, with great difficulty, reads Duʿāʾ al-Nudbah. One who puts much effort into celebrating mid-Shaʿbān, and always speaks to the youth about their master and Imām عجل الله تعالى فرجه الشريف.

Such a person's account is different from the rest. If a person like this told us about the inner reality of the world and the truth of our deeds, he would follow it immediately with, "I say this so that you also elevate [to higher spiritual stations]. Not to rejoice in this world of darkness and deprive yourself of the great blessing of the universe." Aḥmad Āghā, in his youth and adolescence, had reached a point where he knew the ways of heaven better than the ways of the earth.

Once, we persistently pressed him, "Aḥmad Āghā, have you seen the Imām of the Age عجل الله تعالى فرجه الشريف?" As always, he shrewdly avoided this question. He responded with superficial answers that we should all obey the orders of the Imām عجل الله تعالى فرجه الشريف and suggested that visions are not a sign of perfection. Our minds were not ready to comprehend such matters at that time.

***

Once, we went to Qom and Jamkarān for ziyārah with Aḥmad Āghā and the guys of Masjid Amīn al-Dawlah. After completing our prayers in Masjid Jamkarān, we returned to the bus. Aḥmad Āghā came back very casually, like us. The driver told us, "If you want to buy Sōhān (traditional Persian saffron brittle toffee) or go somewhere, you have an hour."

We all started walking towards the shops when suddenly, I saw Aḥmad Āghā heading towards the desert behind the mosque! I called one of my friends and whispered, "Where do you think Aḥmad Āghā is going?" We decided to follow him discreetly.

Back then, things were not like now – the yards were dark and small. Aḥmad went somewhere where his surroundings were getting dark, and we followed. We did not make a single sound. Suddenly, Aḥmad Āghā turned around and asked, "Why are you following me!?"

We were taken aback. I said, "Can you see behind you? How did you notice us?" Aḥmad Āghā replied, "You did not do the right thing. Go back." We insisted, saying, "No, we cannot. We are your friends; wherever you go, we will follow. Also, it is dangerous here; you might be attacked by someone or something."

He said, "Please go back," we replied, "No, we will not return until you say where you are going!" He insisted again, and we gave the same answer. He lowered his head. I told myself, "He must be praying for us in his heart!" Then he looked at us in that darkness and said, "Can you handle it? Can you come with me?" Knowing nothing of Aḥmad Āghā's intentions, we replied, "Tolerate what? Where do you want to go?"

He took a deep breath, then said, "I am going to visit Mawlā (Imām al-Zamān عجل الله فرجه الشريف)." The moment he said those words, my knees gave out. We were terrified. My body trembled. Aḥmad said this, then turned around and continued on his way. As he was walking away from us, he said, "If you wish to come, Bismillāh."

You cannot imagine how we felt. Maybe now I tell myself I should have gone, but fear consumed us then. Trembling with fear, we turned back. An hour later, we saw Aḥmad Āghā returning to the bus from a distance. His face was radiant. He did not speak to anyone and sat down in his seat. From that day on, I tried to be more mindful of my actions. A similar incident occurred once again in the shrine of Ḥaḍrat ʿAbd al-ʿAẓīm Ḥasanī.

***

One of our regular and weekly programs was to visit the martyrs' graves in Behesht-e-Zahrā عليها السلام. We went with Aḥmad Āghā and benefited greatly from it. I remember one Thursday when there were fewer boys than usual. Aḥmad Āghā explained the martyrs' devotion to the Imāms عليهم السلام and the status of martyrdom.

In between Aḥmad Āghā's words, we arrived at the grave of a martyr whom I did not recognize. We sat there. We recited a Fātiḥah. But for Aḥmad Āghā, it was as if he had found his brother's grave—he was in a very strange state! On the way back, I asked softly, "Aḥmad Āghā, did you know that martyr?" He replied, "No." I asked, "Then why did we come to his grave?" But he did not answer. I understood that there must be a story behind this!

I kept insisting. When he saw my persistence, he whispered, "I could smell the scent of Imām al-Zamān ﷻ there. Our master had previously visited this martyr's grave." Of course, he said several times, "If I say these things, it is only to increase your certainty and for you to find assurance in some matters, but do not share this anywhere as long as I live."

Aḥmad Āghā noted such stories in his notebook from last year.

al-Muḥarram

Ustādh Muḥammad Shāhī

On the first night of al-Muḥarram, Masjid Amīn al-Dawlah was covered in black. All mosques were mourning. This was a good tradition among Irānians from the past. There are even narrations that Imām ʿAlī ar-Riḍā عليه السلام covered his house in black on the first of al-Muḥarram.

He always advised, "If you want to cry for something, cry over Ḥusayn عليه السلام." Aḥmad Āghā was foremost in this practice. Even if others wanted to do it, he would find his way to them and put up black covers with all his energy.

I remember one year when Aḥmad Āghā could not come to the mosque for the first day of al-Muḥarram. The Basīj and mosque boys got busy covering the whole mosque in black. It was noon when Aḥmad Āghā arrived at the mosque. The guys were gathered together. Aḥmad Āghā instantly glanced at the door and the walls before approaching. Then he said, "Guys, good job."

But he lumped in his throat. He continued, "You have done something honorable. Guys, Imām al-Ḥusayn ؑ himself, thank you." Some of them easily overlooked this statement, but I, aware of his [spiritual] status, thought deeply about it. Aḥmad Āghā considered tawassul to the Ahl al-Bayt ؑ, the ark of the salvation of Āghā Abā ʿAbdillāh ؑ in particular, to be the best means of gaining nearness to God ﷻ and seeking forgiveness for sins. That is why he ordered me to recite eulogies for the guys. Every time we went on a pilgrimage to the shrine of Ḥaḍrat ʿAbd al-ʿAzīm Ḥassānī ؑ, he would tell me to sit on the steps in front of the shrine and recite for everyone.

In Aḥmad Āghā's writings, this important matter has been highly emphasized. He even advised turning to the martyr of Karbalāʾ ؑ to dispel the darkness from one's heart and soul. One of the texts left behind in Aḥmad Āghā's diary about Imām al-Ḥusayn ؑ mentions, "On the day of Arbaʿīn when I went to the mourning ceremony, I saw darkness in myself. I witnessed a cage spurring around me and imprisoning me! But when the mourning rituals began, I saw the cage get destroyed."

This is one of the miracles of the gathering of Sayyid al-Shuhadāʾ (Master of the Martyrs). I have often heard him say, "There is a light in the mourning ceremonies of Sayyid al-Shuhadāʾ ؑ, the source of which is the Holy Shrine of Āghā. In these gatherings, it is as if the Imām stands by the door and welcomes his guests."

Among the other infallibles, to whom Aḥmad Āghā often resorted, was the blessed being of Ḥaḍrat Zahra. Her blessed name was always on Aḥmad Āghā's tongue.

It is an astonishing matter for me! Many pious martyrs and seekers of God who left this world with martyrdom had a heartfelt devotion to Umm al-Aʿimmāh (The mother of the Imāms). Aḥmad Āghā says in one of his memoirs, "Thanks be to God, I have a high status with Umm al-Aʿimmāh Ḥaḍrat Zahra."

IRGC[9]

The Family and Friends of the Martyr

It was the end of 1982. Aḥmad was busy studying mathematics at Marvī School. The school contacted his family one day, saying, "Aḥmad has not come to school for many days." That night, after returning home from prayers, he was confronted with many questions: "Aḥmad, why aren't you going to school? Aḥmad, where have you been these past few days?"

And he, likewise, answered very quickly and decisively, "I am seeking knowledge, but the school no longer meets my needs. School has been good for me so far, but it no longer has anything for me! For several days now, I have been attending the sessions and classes of Ḥajj Āghā Ḥaqq-Shinās with the seminary students."

Thus, Aḥmad left formal education at high school and joined the students of Imām Ja'far aṣ-Ṣādiq ﷺ school in pursuit of religious sciences. While studying mathematics in high school, Aḥmad Āghā also studied seminary books alongside his academic studies but now devotes all his time to religious studies.

He was not a traditional seminary student in the sense that he read all the standard seminary books. Rather, he was a

---

[9] The Islamic Revolutionary Guard Corps (IRGC) is a branch of Iran's armed forces, established after the 1979 revolution, responsible for safeguarding the Islamic Republic's values and interests both domestically and internationally.

student under his great teacher. For this reason, Āyatullāh Ḥaqq-Shinās and other great personalities of Amīn al-Dawlah Seminary introduced him to various books to read.

He had a unique study routine. Besides this, I had seen him reading scientific books many times. We never saw him idle. He always had plans for his time and took a certain amount of rest. After that, he would study, do mosque activities, do cultural duties, participate in the Basīj, etc.

Several times at sixteen, he decided to join the frontlines of battle. But because one of his brothers was martyred, among other reasons, his request was not accepted. That was until he made his decision in 1983. He joined the Islāmic Revolutionary Guard Corps (IRGC) to help achieve the revolution's goals and at least have done something. Aḥmad Āghā was immediately recruited by a political unit affiliated with the representative office of the Walī al-Faqīh (Supreme Leader) in the Irānian Revolutionary Guard Corps (IRGC).

I remember him saying, "We are in a group that is under the supervision of Āyatullāh Maḥallatī," and he also spoke highly of him. Aḥmad Āghā started working in the office of Āghā Muḥammadī Arāghī.

***

I heard that he was working in the IRGC's political unit. I had his work phone number. I called and started messing with Aḥmad Āghā. When he realized it was me, he laughed and said, "My time here is at the disposal of the IRGC. If you need something, we can talk [about it] tonight at the mosque." That night, I went to meet Aḥmad Āghā at the mosque. I knew that the members of the political unit had important intelligence.

I said, "Aḥmad Āghā, tell me some exclusive news!" To spare my feelings, he looked at me and mentioned some important information everyone had heard in the news that day. Aḥmad Āghā spent two years in the political unit of the IRGC. He was not permitted to go to the front lines during this time. However, he obtained the authorities' consent to participate on the front lines and joined as a Basīj member.

Motorbike

The Revolutionary Guards gave Aḥmad Āghā a 250cc trail motorcycle and a letter introducing him to a driving instructor to get his license. The IRGC officials gave him complete responsibility for the motorcycle, meaning he could use it for various personal and mosque-related work and cover all the motorbike expenses.

The motorcycle was quite large, such that Aḥmad Āghā's foot barely reached the ground whenever he stopped. One day, I went to him and said, "We need your motorbike for two hours at the mosque." He handed us the motorbike at two in the afternoon, and we got to work immediately!

It was very fun. Our two hours he dragged on until the evening of the next day! With much regret and shame, I went to Aḥmad Āghā's home. His brother opened the door. I asked, "Can you call Aḥmad Āghā? I want to return his motorbike." His brother went and came back, "You can hand it to me." That night, when Aḥmad came to the mosque, he acted normally, not to mention the motorcycle incident. Later, we learned he was deeply upset about our unreliability. He did not come to the door to receive it so his anger and disappointment could die.

***

Aḥmad remained entirely at his disposal for mosque activities, from fetching lentils for the Duʿāʾ al-Nudbah [program] to other tasks. Once, while accompanying Aḥmad Āghā on a mosque-related task, we needed to head back quickly, so he increased the motorcycle's speed. The street was also empty; if the 250cc trail bike accelerates even a little, it becomes difficult to control.

As we sped down the street, a car on our left suddenly turned right without noticing us, while another car was moving on our right. Our path was completely blocked. For a moment, I thought, "It is over. We are going to crash," and closed my eyes, waiting for the inevitable.

Moments later, I opened my eyes to see Aḥmad Āghā continuing to drive! I did not consider there to be a one-percent chance for us to get out of that scenario in one piece.

Shaken, I asked, "What happened? Are we alive?" Aḥmad Āghā replied, "Thank God."

Later, when we discussed that moment, he told me, "God helped us cross. We should have had an accident there. But it was God alone who saved us. I lost control of the bike at the last moment and just said, 'God.' Then I saw us easily passing through between those two cars!"

The Summer of 1985

Ustādh Muḥammadī Shāhī and the Martyr's Brother

They had threatened him, saying they would assassinate him. They even called his workplace and said, "We will kill you!"

He came to the mosque and talked to the guys. It was early summer in 1985. At that time, Aḥmad Āghā was at the peak of spirituality. After the lecture, he told me and one of the guys about God's ﷻ decree, "It appears that God has ordained for my martyrdom. [It will be in] one of these next few days!" We were very surprised. At that time, we were fourteen years old. "What does that mean, Aḥmad Āghā? You are not even on the front lines!"

He said, "Yes, but I will be martyred in Tehrān at the hands of the Munāfiqīn (the hypocrites)." We had complete trust in Aḥmad Āghā's words. For this reason, we were very upset. We waited for bad news every day. When our eyes fell on Aḥmad Āghā in the mosque at night, we breathed a sigh of relief and uttered, "Thank God."

Then, one night after prayer, when he saw the distress on my face, he said to me, "Do not be upset. Divine destiny has changed. I am not going to be martyred for now. I will be with you all a few more months." You do not know how happy this news made me. Later, I heard from Aḥmad Āghā's brother that this matter was very serious, so Aḥmad Āghā was ready and armed in the neighborhood for several days.

Masjid Amīn al-Dawlah was strange during the Ramaḍān and summer of 1985. The sound of the munājāt (whispered prayers) of the late Sayyid 'Alī Mīrḥādī, the self-development speeches of Ḥajj Āghā Ḥaqq-Shinās, living next to Aḥmad Āghā, and so on all created conditions that became one of the most memorable periods of my life. I will give whatever God ﷻ wants to experience those radiant days again.

After breakfast, we would come to the mosque and recite the Noble Qur'ān with Aḥmad Āghā after prayers. At that time, it was just me and him. Much of his advice was given during those luminous mornings. Aḥmad Āghā's spiritual state changed significantly in the summer and early autumn of 1985. His prayers had become stranger than before. During congregational prayers, his face would be wet with tears, and his body trembled intensely.

He was like a bird that was no longer able to stay in the cage of this world. I asked myself, "How does Aḥmad Āghā wish to live after this?" At that time, whenever I spoke about miracles or observing the deeds of people, he responded less and said, "For someone who wants to move towards God, these issues are like pebbles on the path." He also gave examples of God ﷻ granting certain seekers of the spiritual path and blessings to pious individuals, such as Barzakhī eyes or Ṭayy al-ʿArḍ (folding up of the earth or covering long distances in the twinkling of an eye). However, they begged God ﷻ to take those things away from them! Because these things are not signs of human perfection!

Aḥmad Āghā would say, "Our grand scholars are [more] interested in living a normal life like other people." I remember he used to say, "This Ṭayy al-ʿArḍ that some people wish for is one of the first things that a believer can do, but the spiritual wayfarers do not even ask God for this!"

I remember Aḥmad Āghā had started wearing glasses. I said, "Well, you should read the Noble Qur'ān more. They say whoever reads the Noble Qur'ān, the problems and pain of his eyes will disappear." He smiled and said, "I know that if I read the Noble Qur'ān to heal my eyes, the weakness of my eyes will certainly disappear."

Then he continued, "I do not want to read the Noble Qur'ān with this intention; I want to have a normal life!" That luminous period passed very quickly. With the arrival of autumn, schools reopened, and my beautiful summer came to an end. But I did not know these were my last opportunities with Aḥmad Āghā.

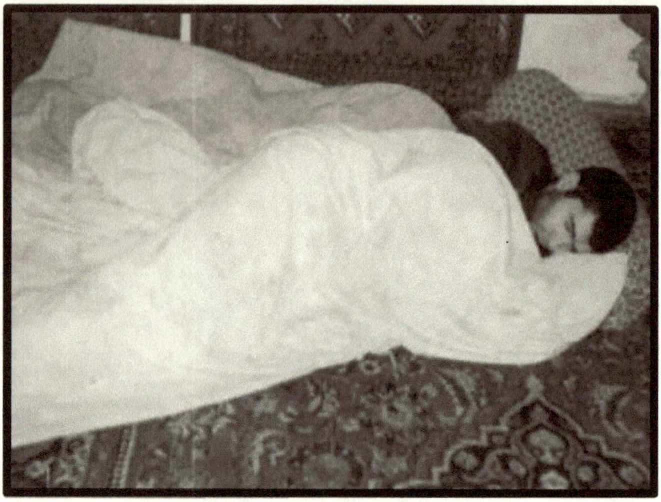

Characteristics

The Martyr's Friends

Our Islāmic teachings teach us that the paths to God ﷻ are as many as the number of people on earth. Man can walk the path to God ﷻ faster and more accurately based on his unique qualities and talents. These unique qualities are referred to as the "character keys." When these attributes blossom, and the keys to good character are discovered, the lock of human life is opened, and man flies to his God ﷻ.

Three decades after Aḥmad Āghā's martyrdom, his character keys can also be analyzed. After hearing the memories of Aḥmad Āghā, many people have become interested in hearing about the unique personality traits of this sincere servant of God ﷻ. To them, Aḥmad Āghā was a very reserved man, meaning he did not talk about his inner [spiritual] states. He, who had reached the highest levels of mysticism and gnosis, behaved like the simplest people so that no one would know about his inner state.

The secret is this: a human with a passion for God ﷻ hides all his inner states and understandings, but God ﷻ places his love and greatness in the hearts [of others].

Many did not witness anything special from Aḥmad Āghā. They loved his prayers, good morals, humility, and so on. He had conquered hearts. He had taught others that one should live a normal life, live like others, be among people, but [simultaneously] be with God ﷻ. Aḥmad Āghā recorded some of his reflections on paper to act as a reminder and shared them with some of his close friends so that they may take a step in that direction.

Sometimes, when he mentioned divine blessings [given to him] to his close friends, he immediately emphasized, "Do not share this with anyone as long as I am alive!" As in, it is clear that Aḥmad Āghā wanted Nothing more from his statements than the growth of others. He did not want the journey to God ﷻ to seem impossible to his friends.

And for others to not feel despair over the hardships of the path and the times. And know that the way to reach the Beloved is always open. Another of his characteristics was his diligence and perseverance in the path of God ﷻ. He responded to the call of *tawḥīd* (monotheism) once and remained steadfast on that path until the end of his life.

God ﷻ says,

﴿إِنَّ الَّذِينَ قالوا رَبُّنَا اللَّهُ ثُمَّ اسْتَقاموا فَلا خَوفٌ عَلَيهِم وَلا هُم يَحزَنونَ﴾

﴿'inna lladhīna qālū rabbunā llāhu thumma staqāmū fa-lā khawfun 'alayhim wa-lā hum yaḥzanūn[a]﴾

﴿Indeed those who say, 'Our Lord is God,' and then remain steadfast, they will have no fear, nor will they grieve﴾[10]

Aḥmad Āghā's faith was not temporary. When he made a decision, he acted determined and saw it through. This can be seen in the guys' Friday prayers, Du'ā' al-Nudbah programs, and other activities.

He carried out the work of the mosque with extreme diligence, exerting effort sincerely for God ﷻ. His other qualities include his method of learning and studying. Aḥmad Āghā began his studies very organized and always paid attention to them. He told a friend, "I set aside at least one hour daily for serious study."

Aḥmad Āghā considered understanding one's audience as the criteria for assessing his work in the mosque. When he was with younger people, he acted like them. When confronting trouble-making and naughty individuals, he was very patient.

***

---

[10] Sūrat al-Aḥqāf, Verse 13.

His most prominent attributes were politeness, kindness, and humility. No one had seen discourtesy from Aḥmad Āghā. His respect, humility, and kindness were well known amongst the guys of the mosque. He treated them very politely. He never diminished anyone's importance in his presence. Seeing him being harsh with anyone, especially teenagers, was impossible. His greatest attraction was his politeness and kindness. He stood up for all newcomers and showed them respect. To encourage the guys, he gave them gifts, most of which were books.

We never saw him forcing anyone on religious and spiritual matters; rather, he spoke so lovingly about the beauty of religious practices that everyone wanted to follow suit. If someone cracked a joke, he laughed along but showed no tolerance for disobedience and sin. Everyone knew that if someone gossiped about someone in the presence of Aḥmad Āghā, he would confront them.

In addition to these qualities, one must mention his reverence for the Noble Qur'ān and the Ahl al-Bayt عليهم السلام. Aḥmad Āghā was very committed to tawassul (seeking intercession). Regarding the Noble Qur'ān, he never forgot to read it attentively every day and emphasized its importance in his will. When these qualities are combined, they showcase the beautiful and pure face of Aḥmad Āghā, a youth obedient to Ḥaḍrat Ḥaqq (God ﷻ), living amongst us with simplicity.

Deployment

Dr. Muḥsin Nūrī

The group of soldiers moved by a marsh toward a field. It was night, and the sky was very dark. Aḥmad Āghā was positioned at the front of the group. As I was looking at them, a mortar shell exploded next to the soldiers! The shrapnel only hit one person. Aḥmad Āghā's heart was the target! He then turned to his right and uttered words I could not understand.

At that moment, Aḥmad Āghā became a martyr before my eyes—and at that moment, I woke up startled from my sleep. My body trembled for a few minutes. The next day, I saw Aḥmad Āghā at the mosque. I described my dream to him. He smiled and said, "I will tell you whether the dream was real!"

It was the autumn of 1985. Changes in Aḥmad Āghā's behavior and actions became more noticeable. All his prayers had become a point of ascension. I remember once, after prayers, I asked him, "What is the reason for all this trembling during your prayers? Do you need to see a doctor?" He replied, "No, it is nothing."

But I knew why he was like that. In the narrations, I read that when in prayer, our Imāms ﷺ trembled like this in the presence of the greatness of Ḥaḍrat Ḥaqq. This state is natural for someone who understands that his insignificant existence has been permitted to speak to the Creator of the heavens and the earth. We must have the necessary maʿrifah (recognition) in prayer and worship. In short, our routine continued as usual until he came to the mosque one night and gathered us all after the prayers.

Then, he said his goodbyes to the boys, "In shā'Allāh, I will be heading for the frontlines tomorrow." Aḥmad Āghā asked us for forgiveness and bid farewell to the mosque community. Then he told a few of us closer to him than the others, "This is my last meeting with you guys. I will not return from the frontlines!" Finally, he looked at me and said, "Your dream was the exact truth."

The guys and I were very casual about it. We thought he would come back and visit during his leave. We thought that even if Aḥmad Āghā left, someone else like him would come along. I do not know why we did not react. We said our goodbyes to him very easily and asked for forgiveness. Aḥmad Āghā settled his affairs with the IRGC the next day and took off for the frontlines as a Basīji. He handed over all the duties of the mosque as well. He had Nothing left to do in Tehrān anymore.

Aḥmad Āghā's letters alone revealed that he was a soldier in the Salmān Battalion of the 27th Division of the Prophet ﷺ.

Salmān Battalion

ʿAlī Mīrkiyānī (Battalion Commander) and One of the Battalion Soldiers

In the fall of 1985, we were deployed along with the battalion forces to the Mehrān region for defensive operations. Our battalion was sent to this city to maintain the security of the Mehrān region. Our battalion consisted of 450 personnel from the Basīj and IRGC forces. While in the area, we were busy training the forces in combat skills for future operations.

Our stay in the western region lasted only a short time. After some time, we moved to Dokūheh. The three-month period of our battalion's rotation we had come to an end. All personnel were supposed to settle their affairs and leave. Given the start of Operation Valfajr 8 in the Fāw region, I spoke to the fighters.

I said, "You can leave now. Your paperwork to leave is ready, but the army needs personnel for the next operation. Anyone can stay." Some of the guys left for personal reasons and difficulties, but most soldiers, including Aḥmad ʿAlī Nayrī, remained in the unit. Although I did not know him at all, nor do I know him now!

We headed for operational duties in the Fāw region. The work in this area was very challenging. ʿIrāq, with the help of Western and Eastern experts, had created the most severe obstacles for our soldiers. Crossing the Arvand River under those conditions and overcoming various obstacles on the enemy's coast was a task that would be impossible without reliance on God ﷻ and the power of faith.

Many military experts around the world still wonder how our fighters crossed the Arvand and reached ʿIrāqi positions. We participated in one of the phases of the operation. Our fighters' main battle with the ʿIrāqi Republican Guard Brigade continued fiercely beside the salt factory. Our unit was given an important mission. We had to go to the Khūr ʿAbdullāh area on the night of the 27th of Bahmān, a week after the start of the operation.

We took advantage of the darkness of the night and transferred a group of troops from beside the marsh and from the Khūr ʿAbdullāh road towards the important bridge in the area. During the journey, several artillery shells landed near our unit. We gained a few martyrs and casualties, but we managed to reach Khūr ʿAbdullāh and commence the attack. Of course, the other guys, especially those in the same group as Brother Nayrī, have more information about him.

A Complete Human

One of the Martyr's Friends

At the age of nineteen, I went to the front lines. I was looking for an acquaintance in Dokūheh. After prayer, I came out of the Ḥajj Hemmat Ḥusayniyah. The face of a young man seemed familiar to me. I approached and greeted him. "I think I have seen you in the ethics classes of Ḥajj Āghā Ḥaqq-Shinās." He greeted me warmly and said, "Yes, I am at your service." This was the beginning of my acquaintance with someone who changed the path of life for many people like myself. Aḥmad Āghā became friends with me from that day on and tried his best to guide me.

I noticed he had very special [spiritual] states during prayer times. I liked to accompany him and benefit more from his spirituality. He would speak to me after prayers. He had good advice. He had a strange eagerness to guide people towards God ﷻ but never liked to play the mentor role.

He told me about the first days he set foot on the path of spiritual wayfaring—how he became acquainted with spirituality and never abandoned his night prayers since he was a teenager! He spoke of acting on religious commandments, that by relying on God ﷻ (tawakkul) and seeking intercession from the infallible (tawassul), one can reach high levels of spirituality. He once said to me, "If someone is careful and does not sin for three days, God will show them the first sources of contact with Imām al-ʿAṣr عجل الله تعالى فرجه الشريف, and if this abstinence lasts for seven days, they will see better things in their dreams until they also actualize for him in reality."

To emphasize the importance of self-development, he mentioned strange things to me. He used to say, "There are those who, after a period of self-development, ascend in their prayers. They detach their souls from their bodies and journey through the metaphysical world during prayer. They even see their body from above!" He mentioned these things, and I was sure he had experienced them firsthand. I once asked Aḥmad Āghā, "Have you seen Imām al-ʿAṣr عجل الله تعالى فرجه الشريف? What does he look like?" He only needed to answer this question properly and change the topic!

But the important point during all this time that I was friends with Aḥmad Āghā was that he was a comprehensive and complete person. There was no negative aspect in his behavior and morals. He never assumed the appearance of a mystic in front of others. He was present at gatherings, and he socialized with others. In social matters, he was like the most ordinary of people. He was a rational person. His actions were based on thought and wisdom.

These qualities made him a role model in the eyes of his friends. Our battalion went to Kārkhah, and Aḥmad Āghā stayed in Dokūheh. He regularly wrote letters to me and used this opportunity to guide me. I remember he strongly emphasized attending the gatherings for the Ahl al-Bayt so that one's inner light could increase since attendance in these meetings has an important effect on the spiritual growth of human beings.

I last saw him next to the Ḥajj Hemmat Ḥusaynīyah in Dokūheh. He took my hand and pointed to himself, joyfully saying, "Soon, the bird will be released from the cage. Soon, I will leave this world as a martyr." He would speak, and I would cry.

I heard the news of his martyrdom a few days later, after Operation Valfajr 8. When I went to Ḥajj Āghā Ḥaqq-Shinās' sessions, he said on the pulpit, "May I be sacrificed for that youth whose prayer was an ascension. In the qunut of the prayer, he went to the kingdom of the heavens. He witnessed the Day of Judgement and the accounting of deeds. He was engaged in true prayer while everyone else prayed the exterior prayer [only]." Ḥajj Āghā did not mention anyone by name, but everyone knew he was talking about Aḥmad Āghā.

Dokūheh

Raḥīm Ithnā ʿAsharī

It was the autumn of 1364 when I and my friends were deployed to the region. Upon entering the Dokūheh garrison, we were divided and assigned to the Salmān Farsi Battalion. This battalion was not permanent; it was formed when many troops were deployed and disbanded when the number of troops decreased. Our battalion commander was Mīrkiyānī's brother, and his deputy was Martyr Muẓaffarī. I went with thirty other people to the second division of the third platoon of this battalion. The commander of our battalion was Martyr Ṭabāṭabā'ī. We had some excellent young men from northern Tehrān, such as Brothers Mīrzā'ī and Ṭalā'ī.

We formed a good group and were stationed in two rooms on the first floor of the Salmān Battalion building in Dokūheh. During the first few days, I realized that one of the youths had a special [spiritual] state. They called him brother Nayrī. In those days, everyone was spiritual, but his state was different! When we discovered he had been one of Āyatullāh Ḥaqq-Shinās's students, we asked him to lead our congregation [in prayer].

Although he insisted a great deal not to undertake this responsibility, he was forced to by the commander. Obedience to the commander was mandatory. In short, the guys in our group benefited from his presence for three months. Brother Nayrī was a quiet and calm individual. Therefore, it took work to understand his character. Most of the time, when we were busy talking, laughing, resting, and so on, he was reciting the Noble Qur'ān or studying. Among our group, one individual spent more time alone with Brother Nayrī than others. They were engaged in spiritual wayfaring with one another.

ʿAlī Ṭalāʾī stayed on Aḥmad Āghā's side. They were confidantes to one another. Ṭalāʾī was the only son of a family from northern Tehrān. He had been raised in a prosperous family that we later found out was not very religious! This is how he arrived, and God ﷻ appointed Aḥmad Āghā for him so they may walk the path of perfection together. Even though he was a few years older than Aḥmad Āghā, they were like Murād and Murīd (teacher and student). He knew Aḥmad Āghā better than others, so he never separated.

Once, we went to visit a shrine together and returned on foot. We were on our way when the guys started speaking to Brother Nayrī. There, the topic of martyrdom came up. The leader of our platoon mentioned the time and manner of his martyrdom! I listened with intrigue. Aḥmad Āghā also said, "I had a dream about my brother. He came after me and led me to the sky. Although, that will not be for a while!" ʿAlī Ṭalāʾī also said, "I am waiting for a shell to explode near me so that I can be reunited with the hoor al-ayn!" Ṭalāʾī had insightful information about Aḥmad Āghā's inner [spiritual] state. He knew things that no one else did. That is why he always stayed on Aḥmad Āghā's side. Once, when they were reciting the Noble Qurʾān together, I sat between them, and the photographer took a picture of us. That became the opening scene of this story.

We were in the Fāw region when Aḥmad Āghā was martyred. Ṭalāʾī was also wounded that night. After the operation, I saw our [old] friends gathered together talking about Aḥmad Āghā. They said unbelievable things! From Aḥmad Āghā's constant connection with Imām al-ʿAṣr عجل الله تعالى فرجه الشريف (or information about certain things, etc.) I told my friends, "We should ask ʿAlī Ṭalāʾī about these cases. He knew Aḥmad Āghā better than anyone else." An old friend asked, "Do you want to see ʿAlī Ṭalāʾī?" I nodded in agreement.

My Friend said, "Good luck. ʿAlī Ṭalāʾī became a martyr in the Fāw region a few days ago and left to join Aḥmad Āghā."

The Lantern Breakfast

Raḥīm Ithnā ʿAsharī

After being stationed in Dokūheh, it was announced that the Salmān Battalion would be deployed to the Mehrān region for defense. I remember vividly that on December 27, 1985, we went to the Sang Shekān area near Mehrān. Overnight, we replaced another battalion. I, Aḥmad Āghā, ʿAlī Ṭalāʾī, and several others were in a bunker. I recall that from the very first day, Aḥmad Āghā intensified his efforts in self-discipline. After the night prayer, he would go to the boys' quarters. He would gently wake them up for the morning prayer.

Aḥmad Āghā would go to the boys' beds and gently massage their shoulders, saying softly, "So-and-so, it is time to wake up. It is time for the morning prayer." Even though they were awake, some boys pretended to be asleep so that Aḥmad Āghā would massage their shoulders! Once everyone was awake, we would prepare to pray. Our bunker was large, and Aḥmad Āghā led the congregation at the front.

After the prayer and recitation of Ziyārat 'Āshūrā', Aḥmad Āghā would set up the breakfast spread and say, "Sleeping during dawn is makrūh. Let us have breakfast." We ate breakfast under a lantern – we called it the "lantern breakfast" those days because it was not yet dawn.

When the sky brightened, we prepared to rest. It was the era of defense, and we needed more to do. Only a few people were on watch duty.

***

A terrifying explosion was heard one day as we sat in the bunker. We rushed outside. A cannonball had hit the area near our bunker. I said, "Guys, could the enemy be trying to advance?" There was a small observation post nearby, on a hill. Our platoon leader and two others ran towards the observation post. Aḥmad Āghā, who was usually quiet and spoke softly, suddenly yelled, "Stop! Do not go there!" All three of them stopped in their tracks. Aḥmad Āghā slowly lowered his head. We all looked at each other in surprise! What did Aḥmad Āghā say? Why did he yell? Suddenly, there was another terrifying explosion sound. Everyone dropped to the ground!

When the dust settled, we looked towards the site of the explosion. The small observation post was gone!

Once, we were heading to the frontlines from afar. A barricade had been set up towards the front line. Aḥmad Āghā moved from the top of the barricade. We descended from the bottom.

The company commander was watching from a distance. Suddenly, he shouted, "Brother Nayrī, come down. You might be shot."

Aḥmad Āghā quickly descended from the top of the barricade. Standing beside me, he said, "Nothing will happen to me in this area. The place of my martyrdom is elsewhere!"

A few days later, I saw him looking very happy. Surprised, I asked, "Brother Nayrī, I have never seen you this happy."

He replied, "I was looking for a book in Tehrān but could not find it. But here, I managed to find this book." Then he raised his hand, holding a copy of the book *Sīāḥat-e-Gharb*.[11]

---

[11] *Journey of the Unseen World*, by Āghā Najafī Qūchānī.

The Last Saga

Raḥīm Ithnā ʿAsharī

I am thankful to God ﷻ. In those days, I had a notebook where I recorded the smallest events. It has been about three decades since then, but it feels like it was only yesterday...

In mid-February, we returned from the Mehrān defense zone to Dokūheh. Everyone could sense that an operation was imminent. Brother Muẓaffarī, the battalion's deputy, spoke to us one night.

He said that with the end of your time on the front lines, you can settle your affairs and return [home], but an operation is imminent. If you stay, it is better. Most of the boys said they would stay, but a few of us left. Our battalion was purified because those who left had no scent of spirituality!

I remember that on February 6, they took us to the operational camp. We were there for a week. On February 9, we heard about the start of Operation Valfajr 8. Two days later, we went to Ābādān.

The next day, they took us to a hangar near Arvand. On February 13, we were transferred to the other side of Arvand. We spent two nights in support bunkers.

We were told that the second phase of the operation was underway and that this phase was much more difficult than the initial attack because the enemy was on full alert.

It was the night of February 16. Brother Nayrī wrote his will.

During dinner, he opened a pack of sweet ḥalwā and said, "Guys, come let us eat our sweets before martyrdom!"

After the Maghrib and 'Ishā' prayers, we prepared to move out. The battalion commander and the axis commander spoke to us. They said, "You must start your movement from behind the area of operation. You will advance on the Khūr 'Abdullāh road. You will pass through the swamp and bypass the Ḥamzah battalion positions. Further on, you will reach an important bridge. This bridge must be destroyed because, in the continuation of the operation, there is a possibility that enemy armored forces will surround our forces by crossing this bridge."

The commander's speech ended. But given the enemy's vigilance and the intensity of the fire, our chances of success were slim. For this reason, another battalion was prepared to support our battalion.

I felt bad inside. Our group leader turned to me and said, "Do you want to become a martyr?"

I said, "Whatever God wills. I came here to fulfill my duties."

He said, "Nothing, then. Be certain you will not become a martyr. One must beg for martyrdom. Someone is not martyred just like that."

The battalion started to move. No one knew what would happen in the next few hours. Our battalion reached the Khūr ʿAbdullāh road by passing through the groves. The movement of forces one behind another in a column began.

Brother Mīrkiyānī was a wounded veteran and could not keep up with the boys, so Brother Muẓaffarī led the battalion.

We reached the positions of the Ḥamzah Battalion soldiers. The shelling around us intensified. Most of the shells hit the swampy area and did not explode!

That night, a group of thirty of us advanced at the head of the battalion column. Brother Nayrī, the platoon commander's deputy, was ahead of the others. We passed through this stage safely.

Martyrdom

Raḥīm Ithnā ʿAsharī

In the dead of night, we approached the enemy bases silently. I could hear the voices of the ʿIrāqis. Under the lights, the enemy machine guns on both sides of the road were visible to us.

My breath was trapped in my chest. The boys arrived individually, sitting in a row behind each other.

I remembered about an hour before [the operation] when all the boys were seeking forgiveness from each other. Which of them will leave to meet their Mawlā (master) tonight? Lost in these thoughts, a bright light lit up above us! An ʿIrāqi machine gunner shouted, "Qif! Qif!" (halt!)

Everyone hit the ground. Chaos ensued. Both enemy machine guns unleashed a barrage on our boys.

The intensity of the fire was immense. The cries and moans of the boys grew louder with every passing moment. I raised my head amidst the chaotic scene. I saw Brother Nayrī kneeling, taking aim with his Kalāshnikov at the machine gunner on the left. He fired several shots. Suddenly, the enemy machine gun fell silent!

Brother Muẓaffarī rushed to the front of the platoon and shouted: "Boys, Imām al-Ḥusayn ﵇ is waiting for you! Allāhu Akbar!" He fired towards the enemy and started running. Everyone got fired up. Suddenly, we all rose and followed him. The enemy line was broken.

The boys quickly advanced towards the bridge, but there were too many enemy obstacles. The conflict intensified. Bullets, shells, and flares rained down on us. We reached close to the important bridge in the area.

***

When we were ordered to retreat, the night had yet to brighten. Another battalion had been chosen to replace us and continue the operation.

When the intensity of the enemy fire decreased, those who were safe emerged from the bunkers. On the way back, I looked at the group of boys. Those who returned were at least sixty! In other words, our three-hundred-strong battalion was reduced to one-fifth its size in less than a few hours!

As we retreated, we arrived at the enemy's gun posts, where our operation began earlier. The body of the ʿIrāqi gunner had fallen to the ground. I had not taken more than a few steps forward when I noticed something beside the road. It was the body of a martyr drawing my attention! I moved forward. My legs weakened. I sat down beside his body. He still had his glasses on. Under the moonlight, his face looked luminous.

It was him—Brother Nayrī—who was ahead of us all in spirituality, the one we never fully understood.

As I looked closer, I saw Mahdī Khodājū's body. Then Ṭabāṭabā'ī, our battalion official. Then Mīrzā'ī. My God, what happened? All the boys of our platoon had gone!

It was as if I was the only one who remained! You could not know how tough those moments were.

When we returned to the base, I searched for the platoon boys. Of the thirty of us who had been together day and night for three months, only eight had returned! You would not know the anguish I felt. I remembered the platoon official's words, "Martyrdom is not just granted to anybody; you have to beg for it."

Later, I heard one of the guys say, "When Brother Nayrī was shot, he fell to the ground. Then he stood up, placed his hand on his chest, and said: 'As-Salāmu ʿalayka yā Abā ʿAbdillāh...' (Peace be upon you, Oh Abū ʿAbdillāh...) Then he fell to the ground and departed [from this world].

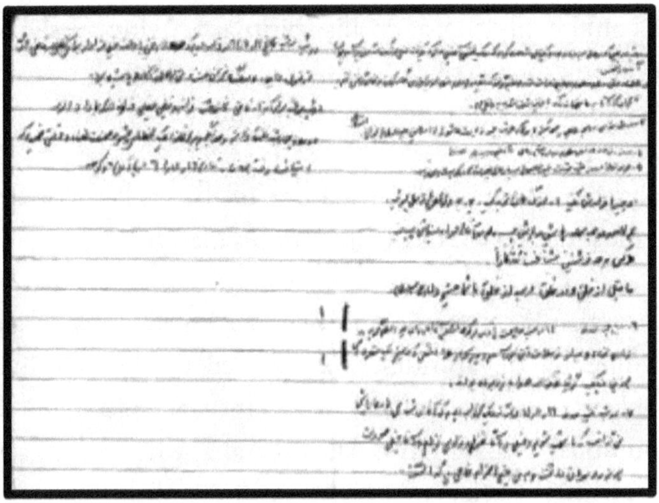

The Timeline of Jihād

The Martyr's Manuscripts and Friends' Memoirs

Aḥmad Āghā's presence on the frontlines lasted up to three months. Just as his rotation period ended and the whole unit was supposed to return, Operation Valfajr 8 began.

Not much is known about Aḥmad Āghā's condition during that time. We tried to find someone who was friends with him on the frontlines but could not find anyone.

We were looking for memories of his time on the front, but we could not find anything because, unlike his friends, Aḥmad Āghā went to a unit where he had no familiar people around him!

No one knew him during his time on the frontlines, so he was comfortable in that regard!

He could easily engage in his spiritual activities, a sign of the people of ma'rifah (gnosis), who prefer solitude and anonymity over fame and presence among friends!

Only after his martyrdom did one of the soldiers come to the mosque and tell us the story of his martyrdom.

Many friends sought to understand Aḥmad Āghā's frame of mind on the frontlines. They used to say: "Ordinary people change dramatically when they are placed in the conditions of jihād. Now, Aḥmad Āghā, who was engaged in spiritual wayfaring of the Awliyā' Allāh (Saints or Friends of God ﷻ) inside the city, what was his spiritual state at the front?"

In one of the letters Aḥmad Āghā sent to his Friend, he wrote:

"The frontline builds humans. The front is a very good place for its people! That is, someone who takes advantage of this opportunity. And it is not a good place for those who cannot!"

The diary left by Aḥmad Āghā, studied after many years, sheds some light on his spiritual state during the jihād. Aḥmad Āghā writes somewhere in his diary, "On Sunday, January 19, 1986, in a stronghold near morning time, I saw in my dreams that Āghā Ḥaqq-Shinās was not permitting us to become martyred due to his supplication. I begged and pleaded with Āghā a lot. Āghā had a very luminous and kind face and treated me with special respect."

Elsewhere, he writes, "On the night of February 3, 1986, I dreamed that Āyatullāh Sayyid Khumaynī was mournfully grieving over Āyatullāh Qāḍī. And this while giving a speech and even...(unclear). That night, I prayed for Āyatullāh Qāḍī, and God عز وجل granted me a great favor at dawn. Alḥamdulilāh (All praise is due to God عز وجل)."

Aḥmad Āghā continues to write in his memoirs, "On Wednesday, I wanted to perform ablution for prayer when suddenly my eyes fell on Ḥaḍrat [Imām al-Mahdī عجل الله تعالى فرجه الشريف]."

Date: 05/02/1986, Dokūheh garrison.

Elsewhere in this diary, he writes, "On Friday, I cried a lot in the majlis of Imām al-Zamān عجل الله تعالى فرجه الشريف, held in the Ḥajj Hemmat Ḥusaynīyah of Dokūheh garrison.

"After *tawassulāt* (seeking nearness to him) and getting a hold of myself, I saw that not a single drop of my tears had fallen to the ground! Perhaps the angels had taken all of it with themselves."

News of Martyrdom

The Martyr's Mother

It had been three months since Aḥmad left for the frontlines. We had yet to hear from him besides a letter or two. I was worried about Aḥmad. I asked his friends, "Have you heard any news of Aḥmad? I am very worried." One day, I saw Radio Māresh broadcasting the operation's advance. My concern deepened. The pounding of my heart was intense. People were happy to hear that the operation had started, but truly, no one could understand the feelings of a mother who had no news of her son's condition. Everyone knew Aḥmad was my best and least troublesome son. I loved him very much. Now, this lack of news worries me a lot. I prayed regularly and thought of Aḥmad—until one night, I saw a white dove perched on my shoulder in a dream. Then another dove joined it, and both flew towards the sky.

I woke up startled from the dream. Could this second bird be a sign of our second family martyr? But no, God ﷻ Willing, Aḥmad will return safely. I fell asleep again. This time, I saw something even stranger. This time, I was sure I would never see my son again. In my dream, I saw that the angels of God ﷻ had come to earth! They were carrying a beautiful room or tent (howdah) that kings used in ancient times among the hands of the angels.

They came near us and put my son, Aḥmad ʿAlī, in it. Then, along with Aḥmad, the angels went up to the heavens. The next day, neighbors came to our house and inquired about Ḥusayn Āghā! It seemed they had heard that Martyr Maḥallatī had been martyred and thought Ḥusayn Āghā was with him. I told them Ḥusayn Āghā was at home. I am worried about Aḥmad ʿAlī. That day, I saw the mother of martyr Jamāl Muḥammad Shāhī. I had known this dear mother for years in this neighborhood. She was looking for Aḥmad ʿAlī. I said, "I have no news. I do not know where he is." She later told me that Sayyidah Khānom, Martyr Jamāl's mother, had also seen a strange dream. She said, "In my dream, we attended the Friday prayers in Tehrān. There were so many people that it was unprecedented. Then they announced that Imām al-Zamān عجّل الله تعالى فرجه الشريف had arrived and wanted to say prayers over the body of one of the martyrs! I moved forward with difficulty. When they wanted to say the martyr's name, I paid attention. It was announced from the loudspeaker: "Martyr Aḥmad ʿAlī Nayrī."

That same day, I saw the comings and goings around our house increase. My son kept coming and going regularly.

It was noon when we heard the news that the plane carrying Martyr Maḥallatī had been targeted, and he was martyred. Then, they came to our house and gave us the news of Aḥmad 'Alī's martyrdom. Āyatullāh Ḥaqq-Shinās attended Aḥmad's funeral and burial ceremony, and the words he used to describe my son made the ceremony very strange. After Ḥaḍrat Āghā performed these rites, Aḥmad's friends came and recounted the miracles they had seen from him. Strangely, my son, who was at home, led a very ordinary life. But I never saw a makrūh (disliked) act from him, let alone a sin!

Aḥmad was gone, but I knew he was not of this world. He was not meant to stay in this world. He was ready to leave at any moment, and God ﷻ called Aḥmad to Him in his youth. After Aḥmad, we gathered everything that he left behind. We handed over several volumes of books to the Islāmic Seminary in Qom. One of the scholars said, "Who were these books for? They are even heavy for the seminary students!"

A Beautiful Scent

Ḥajj Murtaḍā Nayrī

Nawruz (Irānian New Year) of 1986 had arrived. Aḥmad's 40th-day memorial was approaching. So, along with Mājid, we went to order a tombstone. One afternoon, in the middle of the week, we drove to Behesht-e-Zahrā عليها السلام Cemetery. We received the tombstone and aluminum plaque for the grave. Then, we bought some cement and materials and quickly went to Section 24.

No one was in Behesht-e-Zahrā عليها السلام, and it started raining lightly. I thought, "I wish a couple more people had come to help us." At that moment, a young man wearing a green scarf around his neck approached and greeted us. Then he asked us, "May I help too?"

We were happy and said, "Sure, welcome."

As I worked, I reminisced about my memories with Aḥmad Āghā. I was the cousin and son-in-law of their family. We have been together since childhood as well. Whenever we went to the village of Āyīneh Varzān, we were together day and night. Aḥmad was very energetic during his childhood. He easily climbed walls, was good at football, and so on, but when he became a teenager, he found himself on the path of spirituality. Ḥajj Āghā Ḥaqq-Shinās gave good direction to Aḥmad's life and led him to spiritual heights.

They finished placing the tombstone. To install the plaque above the grave, we had to dig a small quantity of the top of the grave to place the plaque's base in the ground. Rain began pouring heavily. The sun was about to set. The soil there was also loose. I sat on the ground and started digging with my hands. A deep hole was made. My hand went into the hole up to the shoulder, pouring out the soil. But I saw a stone blocking my work. My mind was so occupied that I did not realize the hole had gotten so deep that I might reach the grave!

I cleared the area around the stone and pulled it out. As the sun was about to rise, I saw that the space under the stone was empty! I lowered my head in surprise. I saw that the stone in my hand was from the upper layers of the grave, and now a passage had been created into the grave! I became pale. Why didn't I pay attention? Why did I dig so deep here?

As I was about to put the stone back in its place, a delightful fragrance filled my nostrils—a scent I had not experienced again until this day! I wanted to keep my head inside the grave.

I raised my head. There was no scent of perfume outside the grave. The area around the grave had not been decorated with flowers. Only the smell of damp rain was in the air. I said to myself, "Aḥmad was martyred forty days ago. Don't they say that a body begins to smell after a few days?" I lowered my head back inside the grave. It was as if a perfume bottle had been emptied into his grave. We set the gravestone and installed the plaque, preparing Aḥmad Āghā's gravesite for the 40th-day ceremony.

As we were about to leave, I stopped again and stared at his grave. I was certain that Aḥmad Āghā's body remained unharmed and pure, like the other Awliyāʾ Allāh. It had started to rain heavily. I stood there and got drenched. Āghā Mājid called me, and I turned towards the car.

But that pleasant smell lingered in my mind, a fragrance incomparable to any worldly perfume.

Guidance

A Group of the Martyr's Friends

A verse in the Noble Qur'ān says that the martyr is alive. The martyr has power. He can influence, and we see the influence of his blood in society. I first saw Aḥmad Āghā in a dream after his martyrdom. Our friend group had lost its main axis with the departure of Aḥmad Āghā. I became friends with people in our neighborhood who were not tied to religious matters. One night in my dream, I saw we were in the alley with those [non-religious] friends. They told me, "Rasūl, go hide, Aḥmad Āghā is coming."

I went behind the wall and watched from there. I saw Aḥmad Āghā come to our alley with the same radiant and innocent face. Then my friends took Aḥmad Āghā and forcefully carried him out of the alley! As Aḥmad Āghā was being carried out of the alley, he cried, "I must see Rasūl!" There were tears in my eyes. I missed him so much. I ran and jumped into his arms and started kissing Aḥmad Āghā.

I came to understand everything from this sincere dream. The next day, I severed my ties with those friends and never saw them again.

***

I still feel his presence in my life. Even now, I have made my own life and have a child. Even now, when I go astray, he comes to my aid.

I even know some friends whose children have grown up. Aḥmad Āghā's friends' children also connect with him and seek his help. One of our friends had trouble with his son's marriage and asked Aḥmad Āghā for help, and just like when he was physically present among us, Aḥmad Āghā came to his aid!

I even know people born after Aḥmad Āghā's martyrdom and, upon hearing his stories, have fallen in love with him and have a strong bond.

***

Some time had passed since Aḥmad Āghā's martyrdom. We were supposed to go out for fun with some friends, even though I knew they were not good friends and they might turn to sin. God ﷻ is my witness. That very night, I dreamt that Aḥmad had come, and with anger and sadness, he said to me, "Do not go out with them; do not go anywhere with these friends of yours!" The next morning, I told my mother to send them away, no matter what. But I was deeply troubled by what this dream meant! Later, I heard from those same individuals that they had fallen into sin, among other things. Aḥmad Āghā not only cared about our [spiritual] training when he was physically present in the world, but even now, he is still not separate from us and seeks to guide us.

Another friend told me, "During the unrest of 2009, we were confused and perplexed." One night, in a dream, I saw Aḥmad Āghā come to Masjid Amīn al-Dawlah—but he did not attend the prayer! I said, "Aḥmad Āghā, you were not here. Did you arrive late?" Aḥmad uttered one sentence and left, "We are very busy!"

Immediately, it occurred to me that the martyrs solved these problems. I remembered the luminous words of the late Āyatullāh Sayyid Khumaynī قدس سره, who used to say, "The Muslim has been insured and protected by the blood of the martyrs of Islām and the Revolution..."

House of Healing

One of the Martyr's Friends

Āyatullāh Sayyid Khumaynī has a very important and beautiful sentence, "These graves of the martyrs will forever be the houses of healing." As in, they guide future generations to whom to turn to solve their problems in this world and the next. Aḥmad Āghā, as long as he was alive, was like a physician taking the hands of God's ﷻ servants and showing them the path to heaven.

God ﷻ has also addressed the martyrs as living. So, even now, he is seeking to guide. If anyone seeks him out during this time, they will surely not return empty-handed.

Many of Aḥmad Āghā's friends and students never think that he is not among us. They remember him just like before. They talk about Aḥmad Āghā to their children, friends, and acquaintances.

I was always with Aḥmad Āghā until his last days. I remember one day, I complained to Aḥmad Āghā about my mother's illness.

I said, "No matter what we do, my mother does not get better. The doctors have given up hope on her." And then, tears came. Aḥmad looked at my face and said, "Do not worry, your mother will get better!" The next day, my mother was well! She no longer suffered from her illness – until a year later.

A year later, in the last days we were with Aḥmad Āghā, I went to see him again. I was upset because of my mother's illness. He smiled and said, "She will get well, God Willing." And then, very strangely, my mother got well! A year after Aḥmad Āghā's martyrdom, my mother's illness returned. Her condition had worsened significantly. This time, I went to the martyr's grave, situated above the grave of Martyr Chamrān.

I said, "Aḥmad Āghā, may I be your sacrifice. Our mother's illness has been going on year after year! You are alive and aware of everything. Ask God to cure my mother's disease permanently!"" I said this and returned. I felt as if Aḥmad Āghā had smiled again and said, "It will be okay, God Willing." "My mother got better the next day. Even the doctors had lost hope in my mother, but with Aḥmad Āghā's prayer, my mother was cured. My mother did not get sick again for many years after that incident!

***

Every year on the second day of ʿĪd, we visit the homes of the mosque martyrs, especially Martyr Nayrī. This year, one of the young Basījis insisted on coming with us.

When he came to Martyr Nayrī's house, he told me, "I got married eight years ago, but I could not have children." One day, per the advice of the old Basījis in the mosque, I went to Martyr Nayrī's grave in Behesht-e-Zahrā ﷺ.

I had heard he has a great reputation with God ﷻ, so I said, "I believe you are alive and, with God's permission, can solve people's problems." After that, I asked him to pray to God to give me a child. This servant of God ﷻ hesitated momentarily and then continued with a shaky voice, "After that incident, my wife became pregnant, and a few days ago, my twin children were born." There are many such stories that we have heard from friends, acquaintances, and even those who did not know him, but we refrain from talking about them.

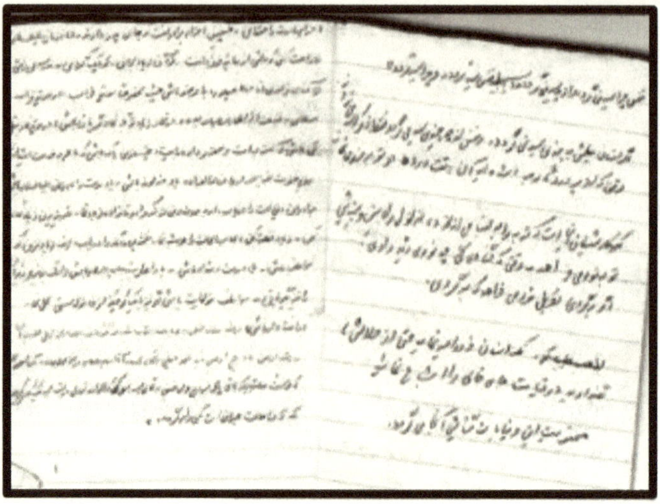

His Will

The mystic and seeker of God ﷻ, Martyr Aḥmad ʿAlī Nayrī, despite spending three months in various operational areas, began writing a will just a few hours before his martyrdom! In the introduction of his will, after praising God ﷻ and offering his testimony of faith, he begins with Āyat al-Kursi and says:

"With greetings and respect to the holy spirits of the prophets and the infallible Imāms عليهم السلام especially Ḥaḍrat Baqīyyatu'llāh (may our souls be sacrificed for him), [I will mention] a few lines from the traditions of the Holy Prophet ﷺ as a reminder for us and me. May they be remnants and enduring [in the afterlife] for me, God-willing.

"ll praise belongs to the Lord of the worlds, who inspired, deemed us worthy, and guided us. And He blessed us with many messengers, especially the Holy Prophet ﷺ and the Infallible Imāms عليهم السلام, so that we may become established guides in this world in the face of the shayāṭīn (the devils, i.e., army of Shayṭān). Blessed are those who have recognized the meaning of their existence in this world and fulfill their duties in the hope of purifying their soul and increasing the degree and pleasure of worship and humility of the heart! Only one who practices strict vigilance over their actions and words can reach such a station.

Qur'ānn, do not forget the Noble Qur'ān. Know that the best means of monitoring your actions is the Noble Qur'ān. Preserve Islām in all its aspects. Help the leadership and Guardianship of the Jurist (Wilāyat al-Faqīh), one of the most important wājibāt (obligatory duties) in this era. May God ﷻ provide you with a good reward! Peace be upon you and the righteous worshipers."

Aḥmad 'Alī Nayrī

2/15/1986

Remembering His Brother

He was a literate young man. He received his university education at Kharazmi University (formerly Tehran University of Teacher Training) in Tehrān. He was deeply religious. That is, anyone who grows up in Amīn al-Dawlah Mosque and is in the presence of Āyatullāh Ḥaqq-Shinās will surely become a complete person. He was athletic and played football for the Tāj (Esteghlāl) youth team. In short, he was the complete package.

During the revolution, Ḥamīd-Riḍā was one of the pillars of the mosque's revolutionary and cultural programs. He was present at all rallies and revolutionary programs. He completed his degree in mathematics and was a student in the field. With the revolution's victory, he formed one of the first student groups to confront anti-revolutionaries. Tehrān Teachers Training University, located on Mofatteh Street, was the center of his and his friends' activities. In his youth, he attended many sessions with scholars such as ʿAllāmah Nūrī and other prominent figures in Tehrān. He thoroughly understood Islām, and no one could shake his beliefs.

I often saw him holding a placard and participating in student rallies. He was among the founders of the Imām Khumaynī Adherents' student group. He would get involved in communist groups and then start debating with them.

No one could counter his strong arguments and rhetoric. He was truly one of the revolution's treasures. Shortly after the revolution's victory, the anti-revolutionaries began to target the university environment.

The conflict was drawn to this environment of science and knowledge. They wanted to capture the Tehrān Teacher Training University in the center of Tehrān. But he did not allow it. With a number of his like-minded friends, he became involved in resistance.

Tehrān Teacher Training University escaped the opposition attack. The same building he protected is named after him: Martyr Ḥamīd Riḍā Nayrī.

The war in Afghānistān began, and our neighboring Islāmic country was attacked. He went to their aid. He said, "Islām has no borders." Along with his cousin, he took off for a foreign land. He returned sometime later, but his cousin Muḥammad Ḥusayn was martyred in the battle. His body never returned. The anti-revolutionaries had made Irānian cities unsafe. He went to the northern regions of the country for publicity campaigns in defense of the revolution. In those years, he had no moment of peace—his heartbeat for the revolution and Islām.

With the start of the war, he bid farewell to his family. He went to Ābādān and joined the army.

But after some time, he separated from them and joined the popular forces under the command of Sayyid Mujtabā Ḥāshimī.

It was the early days of the war, and the operational areas were not very well coordinated. The only organized group was the irregular guerrilla forces operating in Khūzestān.

He joined them and, with his friends, stopped the advance of the ʿIrāqi army. Ḥamīd-Riḍā [finally] attained peace on a cold day in the winter of 1981.

He attained martyrdom after fierce and breathtaking battles on the Ābādān-Mahshahr road.

Ḥamīd-Riḍā's body remained in the operational areas until the next year. With the operation to break the siege of Ābādān, his body was found.

Now, Ḥamīd-Riḍā Nayrī is currently resting near the grave of his brother [Aḥmad ʿAlī Nayrī] in Section 24 of Behesht-e-Zahrā عليها السلام, awaiting the day he rises to aid the awaiting Imām عجل الله تعالى فرجه الشريف.

Letter

One of the beautiful things that Aḥmad Āghā used to do was write letters to his friends and students. These letters were filled with mystical and epistemological guidance. Below is an excerpt from the letter sent to Mr. Muḥammad Shāhī in 1983. However, according to the belief of all his friends, these letters were written with the current generation in mind. So, when you look at these mystical letters, remember that Aḥmad Āghā has written them for us.

In the Name of God, the Beneficent, the Merciful:

﴿وَمِنَ اللَّيلِ فَتَهَجَّد بِهِ نافِلَةً لَكَ عَسىٰ أَن يَبعَثَكَ رَبُّكَ مَقامًا مَحمودًا﴾

﴾*wa-mina l-layli fa-tahajjad bihī nāfilatan laka ʿasā ʾan yabʿathaka rabbuka maqāman maḥmūdan*﴿

﴾*And* keep vigil *for a part of the night, as a supererogatory [devotion] for* you. *It may be that* your *Lord will raise* you *to a praiseworthy station*﴿[12]

A man asked Amīr al-Mu'minīn ﷺ about the reward for praying and reading the Noble Qur'ān at night. He responded,

> "Give him glad tidings, for the one that devotes one-tenth of the night sincerely trying to win the pleasure of his Lord by praying, God will command His angels,
>
> > "write for my servant a reward equal to the number of grains, leaves, and trees on this night, and to the number of seeds, thorns, blades of grass, and bushes..."
>
> whoever devotes one-ninth of the night to prayer, God will grant his duʿā's (supplications), and on the Day of Resurrection, his book of deeds will be placed in his right hand.
>
> Whoever devotes one-eighth of the night to prayer, on the Day of Resurrection, will be risen from his grave with his face illuminating like the moon on the night of the 14th (clear and bright) and will

---

[12] Sūrat al-Isrā', Verse 79.

pass the Ṣirāt (bridge) with those who have not fallen.

Whoever devotes one-seventh of the night to prayer will be considered among those who repent, and his sins will be forgiven.

Whoever devotes one-sixth of the night to prayer will accompany Ibrāhīm, Khalīl Allāh (the Friend of God), in his special station.

Whoever devotes one-fifth of the night to prayer will be placed among the forefront of the victors until, like the wind, he passes through the Ṣirāt and enters Paradise without any reckoning.

And whoever devotes one-fourth of the night to prayer, not a single angel will remain but that it will envy him for his station, and it will be said,

> "enter Paradise through any of its eight gates."

Whoever devotes one-third of the night to prayer, even if seventy thousand times the weight of his sins were to be weighed against his reward, his reward would outweigh it, and this [act] is better than freeing seventy offspring of Ismāʿīl.

Whoever devotes one-half of the night to prayer will receive a reward equivalent to the grains of sand in the desert, and the least of his rewards is eleven times greater than Mount Uhud.

And whoever stands in prayer for the entire night, reciting the Book of God ﷻ, and engaging in bowing, prostration, and remembrance [of God], he will be given such a reward that the least of its effects is that he will be freed from sins as the day his mother gave birth to him.

And good is written for him in the number of God's creations, and status is given to him to this degree, and so forth, and he will be raised from his grave as one of the believers, and God ﷻ will say to His angels,

> "My angels! Look at My servant who stayed awake for My pleasure one night; place him in the gardens of Paradise."
>
> In Paradise, there are a hundred thousand cities for him; in each city, whatever his heart desires is prepared, sights for him to enjoy will be present, and the unimaginable to the mind will be present.
>
> "And all of this is half of the bounties, plentifulness, and stations of proximity [with God] that I have prepared for him."

O God, the Most Merciful of the Merciful, have mercy on me. A cry arises from among the flames of hell, "Here is Aḥmad Nayrī?"

He is the one who wasted his life longing for yesterday and tomorrow and spent his life in ugly deeds. After this outcry, the guardians of hell, with iron rods in hand and with terrible screams, rush towards me and forcibly drag me towards severe torment, throwing me headlong into the depths of hell. They say to me, "Taste it! You are the same one who considered yourself so dear and precious." And they hold me somewhere as a captive forever, a companion of the blazing fire.

The drink will be fire; the abode is eternal hellfire and boiling water. The blazing flames tear me from my place, but the pit of hell pulls me back into its embrace. My utmost wish is to die, but there will be no relief from death. My feet are bound to my forehead, and my face turned blackened by the darkness of sin, screaming in every direction I turn. Wherever I turn, I cry, "Mālīk (Owner), the promises of punishment have been fulfilled upon me."

"Mālīk, the weight of your iron chains cannot be borne; O Mālīk, the decay of our bodies has turned to ash; O Mālīk, release us, for we shall not return to evil deeds." And then I hear the response: "Ever! Now is not the time for salvation. There is no escape from this position of abjection; do not speak or utter a word. If you escape from here by some impossible chance, you will return to the same ugly deeds you were forbidden from."

After this answer, I become completely hopeless. Filled with deep regret and remorse, I am thrust headlong into the fire—fire above us, fire beneath us, fire to our right, fire to our left, engulfed in flames.

My food is fire; my drink is fire; my bed is fire; my cup is fire, and my clothes fire...

***

With greetings to my dear and esteemed brother Muḥammad Shāhī, I hope you are well under the protection of the Most High and have attained divine knowledge. My dear, as I conveyed to you, a person must get to know the Almighty well. [For] when one gets to know God ﷻ well, they strive for obedience and servitude.

However, some of us have yet to know our Lord well. We think we engage in actions that will draw us closer to God ﷻ, but this is not the case. Instead, we move further away from the divine truth every moment we engage in these actions. So, my brother, every moment we commit these acts, we must evaluate our actions from morning to night or night to morning.

I became very upset with your behavior during our hours together because your akhlāq (behavior) had completely changed.! You have fallen behind. Strive to save yourself. If you act lazily, you will stay caught up. Then, God ﷻ will not bestow His grace upon you as He should. Then, you will succumb to your nafs (animalistic soul) and Shayṭān.

It will require much effort for you to find salvation from their clutches. Strive to return to your former status. The cause of this problem lies in your interactions with women with whom you socialize and in your interactions with brothers who are still immersed in the throes of their nafs. When you spend time with your brothers, instead of learning something from them or teaching them something, you engage in meaningless laughter, idle conversations that entertain you, and futile discussions that further veil you [from God ﷻ].

Or, instead of finding proximity with God ﷻ in your solitude, you spend your time in vain thought. Think for a moment. Take a step back. Remember when you were in Tehrān with your companions and friends, how many favors you had, and how much you remembered God ﷻ? Every day, you would at least learn something new or teach something to someone. But now, no!

Instead of remaining silent while in the company of someone and having Nothing to say, you continuously talk. I am very upset to see you like this. Your behavior deeply saddens me. When [so-and-so] said to me in the car: "He has not spoken to me for a while, and even when I greet him, he does not respond."

Is this how you are? I swear by God ﷻ, if you are like this, you are far from the mercy of God ﷻ. Do you want me to introduce you to him [the one from the car]? He is the one God ﷻ boasts about to His angels because of him. He is the one whom the Imām of the Age عجل الله تعالى فرجه الشريف is pleased and satisfied with. Then why don't you speak to him, even though you are so unfortunate? Instead of boasting that God ﷻ has brought you such a person, you distance yourself from him.

Or are you not ashamed? Are you not embarrassed before God ﷻ, who has placed so much love for you in people's hearts and maintained your respect in their eyes? Indeed, it is a matter of shame. Indeed, it is a matter of embarrassment for you to be like this! Know that if you see him and do not kiss his hand and face and ask forgiveness from him, then I will not fulfill my right to you. Go, feel ashamed...

If you are still separated from him, I will pray to God ﷻ to guide you. Perhaps you will see his status in a dream, and when you understand it, thank God ﷻ for providing you with someone like him. My brother, I hope that the Lord guides you and that you will always have the pleasure of God ﷻ. As I told you in Rīneh Village, you do many immature things beneath you. Reduce them. God Willing, you will be victorious.

Consider whether your words benefit you when there is a veil between you and your Lord. Do not support something that you do not understand properly. When you want to support someone, get to know them well and understand their actions properly, then support them.

Know this: I became deeply upset when I first saw you in Reineh on top of that bridge! Because the light on your face had faded severely, I wanted to advise you but could not. My dear, I read the Noble Qur'ān a lot. Remember to study your lessons. Respect your brothers and your friends. You are wrong to suspect any of your friends. You should always consider yourself smaller than them. As for [so and so], you should go to him, and if you see that he is in error, save him rather than abandon him. Do you see how far behind you have fallen? Are you socializing with someone who is a lover of this dunya (world)? Then, strive to return to your previous status.

Turn the words above into practical action. God Willing, you will succeed, and God Willing, you will be saved from the devil who has captivated you.

Old age and youth came by day and night,

We became night, and then the day arrived, but we did not awaken

On the tablet of sin, we did not write an excuse

Next to the Kabāʾir (major sins), we did not write any good [deed]

(Act on the above lines of poetry)

And peace be upon those who follow guidance.

Your little brother, Aḥmad ʿAlī Nayrī

A Letter to Another Friend

Praise be to God, the Lord of all worlds, and blessings of God be upon Muḥammad and his Purified Family. With greetings to my master, the Imām of the Age (May our souls be sacrificed for him), greetings upon you, dear and esteemed brother.

God Willing, you are well and in the protection of God, performing your responsibilities dutifully and freeing yourself from the burden of the shayāṭīn (demons) from jinn and human beings.

Firstly, my brother, it is a source of great pride for me to have a brother like you and to benefit from your spiritual presence. This divine grace is upon me; thus, I must thank Him. This friendship and brotherhood will benefit both worlds, especially in the hereafter.

I wanted to convey a few words to you in person and benefit from your physical presence, but what can I do when divine decree ordained us to be apart from each other? However, I hope we can be together through other means and treat the pain of sin and distance from God with the blessings of Ahl al-Bayt. So we can protect ourselves and others from this abyss of falling into the world's smire and establish pure and special servitude over our entire being.

My brother! Be aware that there is only spiritual wayfaring when getting up at night [for worship]. My dear, correct your deeds, words, actions, and thoughts so that the favor of the night prayer can be revealed to you, and then you can attain spiritual degrees. This will not be achieved, and you will only reach this degree if someone is watching over you and providing you with guidance and akhlaqīyāt (ethical lessons).

Now [you may] wish to find a teacher or spiritual instructor, for there is latent [potential] inside you. But you can only achieve this by abstaining from the abyss of sin in the first stage. In the second, you abstain from the makroohat (which is not recommended) and doubt as much as you can so that a spiritual instructor may gradually appear for you. (Oh calm soul, return to your Lord, satisfied and content) so that at the end of the path (you enter Paradise), by the will of God ﷻ.

Have you ever paid heed to the plight of our master, the Patron of the Age عجل الله تعالى فرجه الشريف? Do you know that our Master's heart aches due to the calamities of his esteemed ancestors and, on the other hand, due to the deeds of servants? Truly, my brother, are we not ashamed of our actions? Do we not know that we inflict another wound upon his blessed heart with every sinful act? It is truly a place of great shame. Why are we so negligent?

On the one hand, our hearts are longing for our Master, but on the other hand, we cause distress to him. Let us try to reduce the hours of our neglect towards God ﷻ. Consume yourself with the shame of your sins, and do not raise your head out of humility. Do you see how a father distances his son from himself with displeasure and how the son, with sighs, cries, and beauty, goes towards his father? If God ﷻ forbid you find yourself in such a situation, go to God with grief, humility, wailing, tears, and a broken heart, for this act is very valuable for those in need of it and for the one who repents. Note that throughout life, the essence of human pleasure lies in moments when there is no barrier between them and their Creator. Is there any greater pleasure than seeing the Infallible Imāms? And how lamenting and grief-filled they are in their whispers with God. Study the life of ʿAlī b. al-Ḥusayn (Zayn al-ʿĀbidīn), read his prayers carefully, and see what they did.

It is shameful that we consider ourselves lovers and Shīʿah of the Ahl al-Bayt, and we know and call each other by this trait, but in practice, we completely fail their requests [and expectations]. For as long as you can, seek knowledge of Him (God); if you attain knowledge of Him, you will reach the highest degree of servitude. There is much talk regarding this topic, and if I survive and we can see each other in person with Ahl al-Bayt's favor, I will tell you how it is possible to overcome ourselves (the animalistic soul). In the hope of that day, God Willing.

A few words of advice and God Willing, action: Ḥaḍrat Baqīyyatu'llāh (Imām al-Mahdī) said to one of the servants of God, "Take care of your dead and keep their hearts satisfied. As much as you can, recite Sūrat Yā Sīn after the morning prayer, Sūrat an-Nabaʾ after the noon prayer, Sūrat Nūḥ after the afternoon prayer, Sūrat al-Wāqiʿah after the evening prayer, and Sūrat al-Mulk after the night prayer."

Elsewhere, the Imām عليه السلام told one of his companions not to forget two things: repentance [for sins] and seeking our assistance in all your affairs. Try to recite fifty verses of the Noble Qur'ān a day, my brother, so that you can plant the remembrance of God in your being and make your appearance clean and pure.

Throughout your life, the results of your actions are of value to you, so trade well to increase that value. Consider intercession to the immaculate Imāms عليهم السلام obligatory upon yourself and weep and grieve for their absence. On Friday nights, recite Ziyārat 'Āshūrā' because it benefits you. Arrange your work schedule in such a way that your work will be beneficial for you.

If your heart is ever lonely, remind yourself of the conditions of death and the hereafter, for it is useful. Engage with the recitation of the Noble Qur'ān, the supplications that have reached us, the remembrance of God, and good gatherings. Do not forget your associates, friends, and brothers, as they deserve from you. Perform your prayers on time. Attend Muslim congregations, especially congregational prayers. Pray with the presence of the heart.

Finally, know that divine success has been guaranteed for an action I will share with you if I see you. Perform the above dhikrs as much as possible, and only do a few recommended acts [of worship] lest the obligatory slip from your hands. Actions that are sustained but few are better than many inconsistent actions.

And finally, if I have failed you with my shortcomings, forgive me and be satisfied with me, and do not forget the right of our friendship and brotherhood in life [in this world] and after death, and do not forget prayers to pray for goodness.

Peace be upon you and the righteous servants of God ﷻ.

Your little brother,

Aḥmad ʿAlī Nayrī

12/22/1985

www.ingramcontent.com/pod-product-compliance
Lightning Source LLC
Chambersburg PA
CBHW031521120626
46545CB00005B/1947